COPP, CLARK & CO.

(LATE W. C. CHEWETT & CO.)

LITHOGRAPHERS,

Chromo-Lithographers and Engravers,

LITHOGRAPHIC PRINTERS BY STEAM POWER.

CHEQUES,

DRAFTS,

BILLS OF EXCHANGE,

CARDS,

BILL-HEADS,

HEADINGS,

VISITING CARDS,

MONOGRAMS,

LABELS,

SHOW CARDS,

ARCHITECTURAL,

ENGINEERING AND

SCIENTIFIC

DRAWINGS,

OFFICIAL AND

PRIVATE

SEALS AND

PRESSES.

In referring to the above department of our business we take this opportunity of informing our Customers and the Public we have added

Copper-Plate and Seal Engraving

to this Branch, enabling us to undertake under our own immediate supervision every description of that class of work, and we feel confident the quality of the work we have already executed is the best guarantee for good workmanship we can offer to those who may in future favor us with their commands.

17 & 19 KING STREET EAST,

TORONTO.

[576]

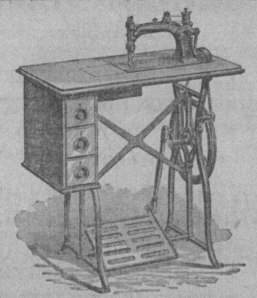

THE BOSS ORGAN!

AT THE CENTENNIAL

THE "DOMINION"

RECEIVED THE HIGHEST AWARD!

INTERNATIONAL MEDAL AND DIPLOMA

FOR THE

BEST REED ORGAN

IN THE WORLD!

The only Organ outside of the United States receiving an International Medal, although seven Canadian manufacturers were competing.

☞ SEND FOR PRICE LISTS.

DOMINION ORGAN CO.,
BOWMANVILLE, Ont.

THE
CANADIAN MERCANTILE
ALMANACK
FOR
1847

THE
CANADIAN MERCANTILE
ALMANACK
FOR
1847

INCLUDING
"TEN REASONS FOR
EMIGRATING TO CANADA"
&
ADDITIONAL 19TH CENTURY
ADVERTISEMENTS

A Canadian Almanac & Directory publication
Copp Clark Professional

Distributed to the trade by
Hushion House
36 Northline Road
Toronto, Ontario M4B 3E2

Publisher: Frederick D. Wardle
Project Editor: Ward McBurney
Editorial Director: Ann Marie Aldighieri
Production Coordinator: Dana Bailey

Design: ArtPlus Limited

ISBN 1-895021-25-1

Canadian Almanac & Directory
Copp Clark Professional
200 Adelaide St. West, 3rd Floor
Toronto, Ontario M5H 1W7
416/597-1616; Fax 416/597-1617
Email: wmcburney@mail.CanadaInfo.com

Printed and bound in Canada

Canadian Cataloguing in Publication Data
The National Library of Canada has catalogued this
publication as follows:

Main entry under title:

The Canadian mercantile almanack for 1847: including "Ten
reasons for emigrating to Canada" & additional 19th century
advertisements

Reprint. Originally published: Niagara, Canada West:
J. Simpson, 1847.
"A Canadian almanac & directory publication".
ISBN 1-895021-25-1

1. Almanacs, Canadian (English).*

AY419.C75C362 1996   031   C96-931959-2

TABLE OF CONTENTS

FOREWORD

The annual publication, *Canadian Almanac & Directory*, has long been recognized as the country's major information sourcebook. This 1,500 page large-format directory is available from booksellers and can be found in most public libraries. 1997 marks the 150th year of uninterrupted publication. In celebration, we offer this facsimile reprint of the first edition together with advertisements and some additional editorial comment from other early editions.

Issued at Niagara in 1847 by John Simpson and the partnership of Scobie and Balfour, the work soon became known as *Scobie's Canadian Almanac and Repository of Useful Knowledge*. 19th century pioneers relied on these volumes as guides to the developing nation.

This 1847 edition includes calendric information and dates significant to early Canadians (Québec was founded on the 3rd of July, 1608; Sir Peregrine Maitland was appointed Lieutenant-Governor of Upper Canada on August 14th, 1818), as well as municipal, school, militia and tariff acts passed by the Upper Canadian parliament in 1846. In addition, Scobie and Balfour appended extensive directory listings for business, government, colleges and the church. Here we find such items as Regulations for Toronto cabbies, "Commissioners for Investigating Losses Incurred during the Late Rebellion and Invasion", and the teaching staff at the Burlington Ladies' Academy, where the Reverend Egerton Ryerson presided over the Examination Committee. Following the appendix are "Ten Reasons for Emigrating to Canada", taken from the Canadian Almanac for 1864.

At either end of the 1847 reprint, we have placed a sampling of advertisements drawn from the Almanac throughout the 19th century. Early Canadian cartoons from *Grip*, "Canada's Comic Weekly", vie with sewing machines, piano and bellows manufacturers, engravers, printers and early photographers, as well as those invigorating and curative electric belts ("Electricity is Life!"). The impressive array of images and typefaces testify to an ambitious lithographic and typographic trade, initially carried out from Scobie's offices on King Street East in Toronto, pictured in the first advertisement shown.

Hugh Scobie stands as one of Canada's most remarkable unknowns. Egerton Ryerson called him "the leading bookseller, stationer, and publisher in Toronto". He was also known as a journalist and editor, and founder of the early Canadian newspaper, *The British Colonist*. Independent of party politics or sectarian interests, save those of the Church of Scotland which Scobie championed in the controversy over Clergy Reserves, the Colonist was "the most distinctive and important journal" of its time in Upper Canada.

Scobie's bias-free almanacs reflect his preoccupation with general usefulness. He was, in his own terms, a "Liberal-Conservative", "neither Tory on the one hand, nor Radical on the other", wishing instead to honour his Monarch and his country. His untimely death from illness in 1854 brought down *The British Colonist*, but his Almanac survived under several proprietorships, eventually becoming, in 1869, the flagship publication of William Copp (who had served as an apprentice to Scobie) and Henry J. Clark, who went on to incorporate the Copp, Clark Company in 1885.

Today the *Canadian Almanac & Directory* is again the flagship publication of William Copp's establishment, now rechristened Copp Clark Professional. From the 1,000 "circulars" that Scobie advertised as having been sent out to update each edition, the current Almanac employs tens of thousands of questionnaires, supplemented by phone calls, faxes and Internet searching, carried out by an editorial team considerably better equipped, but not much larger than the one Scobie assembled in his "Adelaide Buildings" in Toronto.

For our reprint of his earliest efforts, our thanks go firstly to the considerable patience and help from the staff at the Thomas Fisher Rare Book Library at the University of Toronto, where the 1847 Almanac reprinted here is stored, and in particular to the guidance and time of Emrys Evans, Conservator. Michael Cullen of Trent Photographics carefully shot the pages, as well as the accompanying advertisements from later editions, most of which were found through the antiquarian resourcefulness of Michael McBurnie, of McBurnie & Cutler Books in Toronto. Finally, Artplus Design Consultants brought as much clarity and definition to the foxed and darkened 1847 pages as possible.

Leaf through the book. Even if you have only a passing interest in Canadian history, names, places and dates will leap out at you from across a chasm of 150 years, caught in the currency they had during Scobie's early, industrious, and formative time.

Ward McBurney
for the Canadian Almanac & Directory

SOURCES

Campbell, Wilfred, "Four Early Canadian Journalists" from *The Canadian Magazine of Politics, Science, Art & Literature*, Vol. 43, May, 1914, to October, 1914, inclusive; Toronto, The Ontario Publishing Co., Ltd.

The Canadian Encyclopedia, 2nd Edition, Hurtig Publishers, Edmonton, 1988.

Gundy, H. Pearson, *Book Publishing and Publishers in Canada Before 1900*, The Bibliographical Society of Canada, 1965.

Parker, George L., *The Beginnings of the Book Trade in Canada*, U of T Press, 1985.

Ryder, Dorothy E., *Canadian Reference Sources: A Selective Guide*, 2nd Edition, Canadian Library Association, 1981.

THE
CANADIAN MERCANTILE
ALMANACK
FOR
1847,

BEING THE THIRD AFTER LEAP YEAR,
AND THE TENTH YEAR OF THE REIGN OF HER MOST
GRACIOUS MAJESTY,
QUEEN VICTORIA.

NIAGARA:

PUBLISHED BY JOHN SIMPSON; AND SCOBIE & BALFOUR, TORONTO.

PRINTED AT THE OFFICE OF THE
NIAGARA CHRONICLE.

LAW TERMS, UPPER CANADA.

Court of Queen's Bench.

HILARY TERM begins on the 1st and ends on the 13th February.

EASTER TERM begins on the 14th and ends on the 26th June.

TRINITY TERM begins on the 26th July and ends on the 7th August.

MICHAELMAS TERM begins on the 1st and ends on the 13th November.

District Court Terms.

(From the 7th to the 12th December, 1846.)
1st. From the 8th to the 13th March, 1847.
2nd From the 7th to the 12th June, do.
3rd From the 18th to the 23rd October, do.
4th From the 6th to the 11th December, do.

Quarter Sessions of the Peace.

The sittings of the General Quarter Sessions of the Peace, and of the District Courts, commence uniformly throughout Upper Canada on the 5th January, 6th April, 6th July, and 16th November.

Court of Appeals.

1st From the 15th to 20th February.
2nd From the 28th June to 3rd July.
3rd From the 9th to 14th August.
4th From the 15th to 20th November.

Court of Chancery.

1st From the 1st to 13th March.
2nd From the 24th May to the 5th June.
3rd From the 19th to 31st July.
4th From the 6th to the 18th December.

Surrogate Court.

1st From the 4th to the 9th January.
2nd From the 29th March to the 3rd April.
3rd From the 7th to the 12th June.
4th From the 27th September to the 2nd October.

District Councils.

The ordinary meetings of these bodies, by a late Act of Parliament, are held twice a year, commencing on the first Tuesday in the months of February and October.

ECLIPSES.

This year there will be four Eclipses, two of the sun and two of the moon, all of them invisible in Canada.

1. Of the Moon on Wednesday March 31st, visible in the Eastern Hemisphere.

2. Of the Sun on Thursday April 15th, visible wholly or in part at the Cape of Good Hope, Madagascar, Australia, New Guinea, Borneo, Sumatra, Java and the neighboring Islands.

3. Of the Moon on Friday September 24th, visible at California, in the Oregon territory, at Atasha, and in Asia.

4. Of the Sun on Saturday October 9th, visible in Europe, the greater part of Asia, the Northern part of Africa, and the North-Eastern coast of Greenland. This Eclipse will be annular in the South parts of Great Britain and Ireland, and in the North of France.

CHRONOLOGICAL CYCLES.

Dominical Letter,	: : C	Solar Cycle, :	: : 8
Golden Number,	: : 5	Roman Indiction,	: : 5
Epact, : :	: : 14	Julian Period,	: 6560

MOVEABLE FEASTS.

Easter Sunday, :	April 4	Whit Sunday, :	May 23
Rogation Sunday,	May 9	Trinity Sunday, :	May 30
Ascension Day, :	May 13	Advent Sunday, :	Nov. 28

EQUINOXES AND SOLSTICES.

Vernal Equinox, March 21st, 0h. 49m. morning.
Summer Solstice, June 21st, 9h. 35m. evening.
Autumnal Equinox, Septr. 23rd, 11h. 38m. evening.
Winter Solstice, December 22nd, 5h. 21m. morning.

MOON'S CHANGES.

F Moon 1st, 9h 58m mo | First Qr 23rd, 11h 34m mo
N Moon 16th, 6h 1m eve | F Moon 31st, 3h 45m mo

DM	D. W.	REMARKABLE DAYS, &c.	MOON rises	SUN rises	sets
1	frid	Circumcision	rises	7 34	4 26
2	sat	General Wolfe b. 1727 *Snow*	6 8	7 33	4 27
3	A	2nd Sunday after Christmas	7 6	7 33	4 27
4	mon	[3 Battle of Princeton 1777	8 4	7 32	4 28
5	tues	Quarter Ses. & District Court	9 1	7 32	4 28
6	wed	Epiphany. Twelfth day	9 58	7 31	4 29
7	thur	Common Prayer estab. 1549	10 55	7 30	4 30
8	frid	Battle of New Orleans 1815	11 53	7 30	4 30
9	sat	Nelson's funeral 1806 *Windy*	morn	7 29	4 31
10	A	1st Sunday after Epiphany	0 51	7 29	4 31
11	mon	Plough Monday	1 51	7 28	4 32
12	tues	Sir C. Bagot Gov. Gen. 1842	2 52	7 27	4 33
13	wed	[14 Halley died 1742	3 53	7 26	4 34
14	thur	Battle of Rivoli 1797	4 53	7 25	4 35
15	frid	Code Napoleon 1804	5 50	7 25	4 35
16	sat	Sir John Moore killed 1809	sets	7 24	4 37
17	A	2nd Sunday after Epiphany	6 6	7 23	4 38
18	mon	Ciudad Rodrigo stormed 1812	7 20	7 22	4 39
19	tues	James Watt b. 1736 *Moderate*	8 34	7 21	4 40
20	wed	U S. Independence ack. 1783	9 46	7 20	4 41
21	thur	Agnes. Louis XVI ex. 1793	10 57	7 19	4 42
22	frid	Vincent. Bat. Riv. Raisin 1813	morn	7 18	4 43
23	sat	Pitt d. 1806. Duke Kent d. 1820	0 6	7 17	4 44
24	A	3rd Sunday after Epiphany	1 12	7 16	4 45
25	mon	Conversion of St. Paul. Sir F.	2 16	7 15	4 46
26	tues	B. Head Lieut. Gov. 1836	3 16	7 13	4 47
27	wed	Mozart b. 1756 *Symptoms of*	4 11	7 12	4 48
28	thur	Gibbon d. 1794 *a thaw*	5 0	7 11	4 49
29	frid	George III died 1820	5 45	7 10	4 50
30	sat	Lord Metcalfe born 1785	6 21	7 9	4 52
31	A	Septuages. G Fawkes ex 1606	rises	7 8	4 53

| 1847. | FEBRUARY. | 28 Days. |

MOON'S CHANGES.

Last Qr 8th, 8h 55m mo | N Moon 15th 6h 42m mo
First Qr 21st, 11h 15m eve.

DM	D. W.	REMARKABLE DAYS, &c.	MOON rises	SUN rises	SUN sets
1	mon	Hilary Term begins *Snow*	6 52	7 6	4 54
2	tues	Purif. B. V. Mary	7 49	7 5	4 55
3	wed	War decld by France 1793	8 46	7 4	4 57
4	thur	George Lillo born 1693	9 43	7 3	4 58
5	frid	Sir Robert Peel born 1788	10 41	7 1	4 59
6	sat	Duckworth's victory 1806	11 39	7 0	5 1
7	A	Sexagesima *Clear and cold*	morn	6 59	5 2
8	mon	Battle of Eylau 1807	0 38	6 57	5 3
9	tues	[10 Queen Vic, mar 1839	1 37	6 56	5 5
10	wed	Lord Sydenham Gov G 1840	2 36	6 55	5 6
11	thur	Battle Montmirail 1814	3 33	6 53	5 7
12	frid	13 B Cellino d 1570	4 27	6 52	5 8
13	sat	Hilary Term ends	5 17	6 50	5 10
14	A	St Valentine. Quinquagesima	6 2	6 49	5 12
15	mon	Collop Monday *Changeable*	sets	6 48	5 13
16	tues	Shrove Tuesday	7 23	6 46	5 14
17	wed	Ash Wednesday	8 37	6 45	5 16
18	thur	Luther died 1545	9 50	6 43	5 17
19	frid	Dardanelles forced 1807	11 0	6 42	5 19
20	sat	Galileo born 1564 *Snow*	morn	6 41	5 20
21	A	1st Sunday in Lent	0 7	6 39	5 22
22	mon	Washington born 1732	1 9	6 38	5 23
23	tues	Sir J Reynolds died 1792	2 6	6 36	5 25
24	wed	St Matthias	2 57	6 35	5 26
25	thur	Dr Buchan d 1805 *Moderate*	3 43	6 33	5 27
26	frid	Bonaparte left Elba 1815	4 24	6 32	5 29
27	sat	Battle of Orthes 1814	5 0	6 30	5 30
28	A	2nd Sunday in Lent	5 33	6 28	5 32

Venus is Evening Star until October 3rd, and Morning Star from that day to the end of the year.

MOON'S CHANGES.

F Moon 1st, 10h 25m eve	First Qr 23rd, 0h 57m eve
N Moon 16th, 4h 27m eve	F Moon 31st, 4h 33m eve

DM	D. W.	REMARKABLE DAYS, &c.	MOON sets	SUN rises	SUN sets
1	mon	St David	6 3	6 27	5 33
2	tues	St Chad *Cold*	rises	6 26	5 35
3	wed	Battle Point-au-Pelee 1838	7 37	6 24	5 36
4	thur	First American Congress 1789	8 34	6 23	5 38
5	frid	Corregio died 1534 *Change*	9 31	6 21	5 40
6	sat	Battle of Barossa 1811	10 30	6 20	5 41
7	A	3rd Sunday in Lent	11 28	6 18	5 42
8	mon	District Court Term begins	*morn*	6 17	5 44
9	tues	Battle of Laon 1814	0 25	6 15	5 45
10	wed	Botany Bay discovered 1787	1 21	6 14	5 47
11	thur	Tasso born 1544 *High winds*	2 15	6 12	5 48
12	frid	Gregory	3 5	6 11	5 50
13	sat	District Court Term ends	3 51	6 9	5 51
14	A	[13 Priestly b 1733 *Snow or*	4 33	6 8	5 53
15	mon	[16 Boileau b 1635 *Rain*	5 13	6 6	5 54
16	tues	Gustavus of Sweden assass'd	sets	6 5	5 56
17	wed	St Patrick	7 24	6 4	5 56
18	thur	Sterne died 1768 *accompanied*	8 38	6 3	5 57
19	frid	C Le Brun b 1739 *with heavy*	9 49	6 2	5 58
20	sat	Newton died 1727 *gusts of*	10 55	6 1	5 59
21	A	Vernal Equinox *wind*	11 57	6 0	6 0
22	mon	Goethe died 1832	*morn*	5 58	6 2
23	tues	Sir G Arthur Lt Gov 1838	0 52	5 56	6 4
24	wed	[23 Martinique taken 1794	1 41	5 54	6 6
25	thur	Annunciation B V Mary	2 23	5 52	6 9
26	frid	P G Cambridge b 1819 *Milder*	3 1	5 50	6 11
27	sat	Peace of Amiens 1802	3 35	5 48	6 13
28	A	Palm Sunday	4 5	5 47	6 14
29	mon	Sir R Abercrombie died 1801	4 34	5 45	6 15
30	tues	[31 Ld Metcalfe G G 1843	5 2	5 44	6 17
31	wed	Eclipse of the moon invisible	rises	5 42	6 18

1847. APRIL. 30 Days.

MOON'S CHANGES.

Last Qr 8th, 10h 42m mo | First Qr 22nd, 4h 25m mo
N Moon 15th, 1h 38m mo | F Moon 30th, 8h 42m mo

DM	D. W.	REMARKABLE DAYS, &c.	MOON rises	SUN rises	sets
1	thur	Maundy Thursday	7 25	5 41	6 20
2	frid	Good Friday	8 24	5 39	6 21
3	sat	Bonaparte dethroned 1814	9 22	5 38	6 23
4	A	Easter Sunday	10 20	5 36	6 24
5	mon	General Sale's victory 1842	11 16	5 35	6 26
6	tues	Quarter Ses & Dis Courts	morn	5 33	6 27
7	wed	Francis Xavier b 1506 *Cloudy*	0 9	5 32	6 29
8	thur	Lord Bacon died 1626 *with*	0 59	5 31	6 30
9	frid	Badajoz stormed 1812 *showers*	1 45	5 29	6 32
10	sat	Battle of Toulouse 1814	2 27	5 28	6 33
11	A	Low Sunday	3 7	5 26	6 35
12	mon	[13 Handel died 1759 *Mild*	3 44	5 25	6 36
13	tues	Nia. & Mid. Assizes begin	4 20	5 23	6 37
14	wed	Catholic Emancipation 1829	4 57	5 22	6 39
15	thur	Eclipse of the sun invisible	sets	5 20	6 40
16	frid	Buffon died 1788	8 34	5 19	6 41
17	sat	Franklin died 1790	9 40	5 18	6 43
18	A	2nd Sunday after Easter	10 40	5 16	6 45
19	mon	Lord Byron died 1824	11 33	5 15	6 46
20	tues	*Pleasant*	morn	5 13	6 47
21	wed	Span Armada des 1657 *weather*	0 19	5 12	6 49
22	thur	Johnstown Assizes begin	1 0	5 11	6 50
23	frid	St George's Day	1 35	5 9	6 52
24	sat	Shakspeare b 1554 d 1616	2 7	5 8	6 53
25	A	St Mark Princess Alice b 1843	2 37	5 7	6 54
26	mon	[25 Sir G Murray L G 1815	3 5	5 6	6 56
27	tues	Bruce the trav died 1794 *Cool*	3 33	5 4	6 57
28	wed	Gore & Eastern Assizes begin	4 1	5 3	6 58
29	thur	Bp Cooper died 1594 *Change*	4 31	5	7 0
30	frid	Washington President 1789	rises	5 0	7 1

MOON'S CHANGES.

Last Qr 7th, 6h 5m eve | *First Qr 21st, 9h 15m eve*
N Moon 14th, 10h 39m mo | *F Moon 29th, 10h 2m eve*

DM	D. W.	REMARKABLE DAYS, &c.	MOON rises	SUN rises	sets
1	sat	Philip Jas. Wellington b 1769	8 14	4 59	7 2
2	A	4th Sunday after Easter	9 11	4 57	7 3
3	mon	Bat of Fuentes d'Onoro 1811	10 6	4 56	7 5
4	tues	Western Assizes begin	10 57	4 55	7 6
5	wed	Dalhousie Assizes begin	11 44	4 54	7 7
6	thur	[5 Bonaparte died 1821	morn	4 52	7 8
7	frid	Suckling d 1641 *Very warm*	0 27	4 51	7 9
8	sat	*and pleasant*	1 6	4 50	7 11
9	A	Rogation Sunday	1 42	4 49	7 12
10	mon	Brock Assizes begin	2 18	4 48	7 13
11	tues	Bath't & Home Assizes begin	2 53	4 47	7 14
12	wed	Strafford beheaded 1641	3 29	4 45	7 15
13	thur	Lon Assizes begin. Ascension	4 8	4 44	7 16
14	frid	Talbot Assizes begin *Change*	sets	4 43	7 17
15	sat	[16 Battle of Albuera 1811	8 23	4 42	7 19
16	A	Sunday after Ascension	9 21	4 41	7 20
17	mon	*Showers*	10 12	4 40	7 21
18	tues	Bonaparte Emperor 1804	10 55	4 39	7 22
19	wed	Sir C Bagot died 1843	11 34	4 38	7 23
20	thur	Columbus died 1506	morn	4 37	7 24
21	frid	Huron Assizes begin	0 8	4 36	7 24
22	sat	Battle of Aspern 1809	0 38	4 35	7 25
23	A	Pentecost, Whit Sunday	1 7	4 34	7 26
24	mon	Queen Victoria born 1819	1 35	4 33	7 27
25	tues	Irish Rebellion 1798	2 3	4 32	7 28
26	wed	Wel. & Victoria Assizes begin	2 32	4 32	7 29
27	thur	Fort George taken 1814	3 3	4 31	7 30
28	frid	Great Fire at Quebec 1845	3 38	4 30	7 30
29	sat	[William Pitt born 1759	rises	4 29	7 31
30	A	Trinity Sunday	8 0	4 29	7 32
31	mon	*Growing weather*	8 54	4 28	7 33

MOON'S CHANGES.

Last Qr 5*th*, 11*h* 22*m eve*	*First* Qr 20*th* 2*h* 48*m eve*
N Moon 12*th*, 8*h* 8*m eve*	*F Moon* 28*th*, 8*h* 39*m mo*

DM	D. W.	REMARKABLE DAYS, &c.	MOON rises	SUN rises	sets
1	tues	Newcastle Assizes begin	9 43	4 27	7 33
2	wed	[1 Lord Howe's vict 1794	10 28	4 26	7 34
3	thur	Dr Hutton b 1726 *Hot and*	11 8	4 26	7 34
4	frid	Lord Eldon b 1751 *Dry*	11 45	4 25	7 35
5	sat	King of Hanover born 1771	*morn*	4 25	7 36
6	A	1st Sunday after Trinity	0 20	4 24	7 36
7	mon	District Court Term begins	0 54	4 24	7 36
8	tues	The Black Prince d 1376	1 29	4 23	7 37
9	wed	St Anthony . *Frequent*	2 5	4 23	7 37
10	thur	Dolland b 1706 *Showers*	2 45	4 22	7 38
11	frid	St Barnabas	3 29	4 22	7 38
12	sat	District Court Term ends	sets	4 22	7 38
13	A	Lord Bridport's victory 1795	8 2	4 21	7 39
14	mon	Easter Term begins	8 49	4 21	7 39
15	tues	Wat Tyler killed 1381 *Fair*	9 30	4 21	7 39
16	wed	Battle of Ligny 1815	10 7	4 21	7 39
17	thur	Battle of Bunker Hill 1775	10 39	4 21	7 40
18	frid	Battle of Waterloo 1815	11 9	4 20	7 40
19	sat	B de Rottenburgh Pre't 1813	11 37	4 20	7 40
20	A	Q Victoria's accession 1837	*morn*	4 20	7 40
21	mon	Summer solstice	0 5	4 20	7 40
22	tues	[21 Battle of Vittoria 1813	0 33	4 20	7 40
23	wed	[21 B of Vinegar Hill 1798	1 3	4 20	7 40
24	thur	St John Baptist	1 36	4 20	7 40
25	frid	*Look for rain*	2 13	4 20	7 40
26	sat	Easter T ends. G IV d 1830	2 55	4 20	7 39
27	A	4th Sunday after Trinity	3 44	4 21	7 39
28	mon	2nd Great F. at Quebec 1845	rises	4 21	7 39
29	tues	St Peter	8 25	4 21	7 39
30	wed	Sir P Maitland Lt Gov 1820	9 8	4 21	7 38

MOON'S CHANGES.

Last Qr 5th, 3h 58m *mo* | *First Qr* 20th, 8h 8m *mo*
N Moon 12th, 6h 54m *mo* | *F Moon* 27th, 5h 24m *eve*

DM	D. W	REMARKABLE DAYS, &c.	MOON rises	SUN rises	SUN sets
1	thur	Sir F P Robinson Lt G 1815	9 47	4 22	7 38
2	frid	[1 Hull in. Canada 1812	10 23	4 22	7 38
3	sat	Quebec founded 1608	10 58	4 22	7 37
4	A	U S Independence	11 32	4 23	7 37
5	mon	[6 Battle of Maida 1806	morn	4 23	7 36
6	tues	Quarter Ses & District Courts	0 8	4 24	7 36
7	wed	Col. Simcoe Lt Gov 1792	0 45	4 24	7 35
8	thur	*Dry and Dusty*	1 27	4 25	7 35
9	frid	Edmund Burke died 1797	2 12	4 25	7 34
10	sat	Columbus born 1447	3 2	4 26	7 34
11	A	6th Sun after Trin *Thun with*	3 57	4 27	7 34
12	mon	*Showers in*	sets	4 27	7 33
13	tues	Bonaparte surrendered 1815	8 5	4 28	7 32
14	wed	Mrs Siddons b 1755 *var. places*	8 39	4 29	7 31
15	thur	St Swithin	9 10	4 29	7 30
16	frid	Detroit taken 1812	9 39	4 30	7 29
17	sat	Michilimacinack taken 1812	10 7	4 31	7 29
18	A	7th Sunday after Trinity	10 35	4 31	7 28
19	mon	Great fire in New York 1845	11 4	4 32	7 27
20	tues	[21 Robt Burns died 1796	11 35	4 33	7 26
21	wed	Hon P Russell Prest 1796	morn	4 34	7 25
22	thur	Battle of Salamanca 1812	0 9	4 35	7 24
23	frid	Gibraltar taken 1704	0 48	4 36	7 23
24	sat	Duchess of Cambridge b 1797	1 33	4 37	7 22
25	A	St Jas. 8th Sun after Trinity	2 25	4 38	7 21
26	mon	Trin Term begins. St Anne	3 24	4 39	7 20
27	tues	French Rev 1830 *Very hot*	rises	4 40	7 19
28	wed	Talav 1809 ; Sauroren 1813	7 44	4 41	7 18
29	thur	Robespierre executed 1794	8 23	4 42	7 17
30	frid	Dog Days begin	8 59	4 43	7 16
31	sat	St Sebastian stormed 1813	9 35	4 44	7 15

MOON'S CHANGES.

Last Qr 3rd, 9h 15m mo | *First Qr 19th, 0h 17m mo*
N Moon 10th, 7h 44m eve | *F Moon 26th, 1h 25m mo*

DM	D. W.	REMARKABLE DAYS, &c.	MOON rises	SUN rises	sets
1	A	Battle of the Nile 1798	10 10	4 45	7 14
2	mon	Bonaparte First Consul 1802	10 48	4 46	7 13
3	tues	First Voy of Columbus 1540	11 28	4 48	7 12
4	wed	Shelley born 1792 *Showers*	morn	4 49	7 10
5	thur	Battle of Brownstown 1812	0 11	4 50	7 9
6	frid	Transfiguration	1 0	4 51	7 7
7	sat	Trinity Term ends	1 52	4 .52	7 7
8	A	Louis Phil K of the F 1830	2 47	4 54	7 6
9	mon	[8 Canning d 1827 *Pleasant*	3 45	4 55	7 4
10	tues	St Lawrence	sets	4 56	7 3
11	wed	Battle of L Champlain 1814	7 12	4 57	7 2
12	thur	George IV born 1762	7 41	4 59	7 1
13	frid	Queen Adelaide born 1792	8 10	5 0	6 59
14	sat	[13 Sir P Maitland Lt G 1818	8 38	5 1	6 58
15	A	Bonaparte born 1769	9 6	5 2	6 57
16	mon	And. Marvell d 1678 *Dry &*	9 36	5 4	6 56
17	tues	Gen Hunter Lt Gov 1799	10 9	5 5	6 54
18	wed	[17 Fred the Great d 1786	10 45	5 6	6 53
19	thur	Royal Geo sunk 1782 *Dusty*	11 26	5 8	6 52
20	frid	Treaty of Washington 1842	morn	5 9	6 50
21	sat	Battle of Vimiero 1808	0 13	5 10	6 49
22	A	12th Sunday after Trinity	1 7	5 12	6 47
23	mon	[24 B of Bladensburgh 1814	2 8	5 13	6 46
24	tues	St Bartholomew ●	3 15	5 15	6 45
25	wed	F Gore Esqr Lt Gov 1806	4 26	5 16	6 43
26	thur	Prince Albert born 1819	rises	5 17	6 42
27	frid	Battle of Long Island 1776	7 32	5 19	6 40
28	sat	St Augustine	8 9	5 20	6 39
29	A	St John Baptist beheaded	8 47	5 21	6 38
30	mon	Paley born 1743	9 27	5 23	6 36
31	tues	John Bunyan died 1688	10 11	5 24	6 35

MOON'S CHANGES.

Last Qr 1st, 4h 30m eve | First Qr 17th, 2h 37m eve
N Moon 9th, 11h 3m mo | F Moon 24th, 9h 41m mo

DM	D. W	REMARKABLE DAYS, &c.	MOON rises	SUN rises	sets
1	wed	[2 Fire of Lon 1666 *Cool &*	10 58	5 26	5 33
2	thur	Danish fleet surrendered 1807	11 49	5 27	6 32
3	frid	Sir E Coke died 1634 *Pleasant*	morn	5 29	6 31
4	sat	14th Sunday after Trinity	0 43	5 30	6 29
5	A	The Boxer captured 1814	1 40	5 31	6 28
6	mon	Transfiguration	2 37	5 33	6 26
7	tues	Battle of Borodino 1812	3 35	5 34	6 25
8	wed	Nativity B V Mary	4 32	5 36	6 23
9	thur	Battle of Flodden 1513	sets	5 37	6 22
10	frid	Dog D end. Bat. L Erie 1813	6 41	5 39	6 20
11	sat	Hon A Grant Prest 1805	7 9	5 40	6 19
12	A	15th Sunday after Trinity	7 39	5 42	6 18
13	mon	Niag & Western Assizes beg.	8 10	5 43	6 16
14	tues	[Chas Jas Fox died 1806	8 44	5 45	6 15
15	wed	Malta taken 1800	9 23	5 46	6 13
16	thur	*Wind and Rain*	10 7	5 48	6 12
17	frid	Washington retired 1796	10 56	5 49	6 10
18	sat	Moscow burnt 1812	11 52	5 51	6 9
19	A	Lord Sydenham died 1841	*morn*	5 52	6 8
20	mon	*Change*	0 54	5 54	6 6
21	tues	London Assiz. beg. St Matthew	2 1	5 55	6 4
22	wed	[23 Battle of Assaye 1803	3 12	5 57	6 3
23	thur	Autumnal Equinox	4 26	5 58	6 1
24	frid	Midland Assizes begin	rises	6 0	6 0
25	sat	[24 Eclipse of the moon invis	6 40	6 1	5 58
26	A	17th Sunday after Trinity	7 21	6 3	5 57
27	mon	B Busaco 1810. Nelson b 1758	8 4	6 4	5 55
28	tues	Gore Assizes begin	8 52	6 5	5 54
29	wed	Michaelmas Day	9 43	6 7	5 52
30	thur	Brock Prest 1808. St Jerome	10 38	6 8	5 51

| 1847. | OCTOBER. | 31 Days. |

DM	D. W.	REMARKABLE DAYS, &c.	MOON rises	SUN rises	sets
1	frid	Chusan captured 1841	11 34	6 10	5 49
2	sat	Major Andre executed 1780	morn	6 11	5 48
3	A	18th Sunday after Trinity	0 32	6 13	5 46
4	mon	Johnstown Assizes begin	1 30	6 14	5 45
5	tues	Battle of the Thames 1813	2 28	6 16	5 43
6	wed	Prince E Assizes begin. Faith	3 25	6 17	5 42
7	thur	Home Assizes begin	4 22	6 19	5 40
8	frid	*Cold and wet*	5 18	6 20	5 39
9	sat	Eclip of the sun inv. St Denis	sets	6 22	5 37
10	A	19th Sunday after Trinity	6 12	6 23	5 36
11	mon	Eastern & Vict. Assizes begin	6 46	6 25	5 35
12	tues	*Windy*	7 23	6 26	5 33
13	wed	General Brock killed 1812	8 4	6 28	5 32
14	thur	Battle of Jena 1806	8 51	6 29	5 30
15	frid	Joachim Murat shot *Change*	9 43	6 31	5 29
16	sat	Marie Antoinette exe 1793	10 41	6 32	5 27
17	A	[18 Dist Court Term begins	11 44	6 34	5 26
18	mon	Newcastle & Otta A b St Luke	morn	6 35	5 24
19	tues	[18 Battle of Leipsic 1813	0 51	6 37	5 23
20	wed	[21 Lord Nelson killed 1805	2 0	6 38	5 21
21	thur	Simcoe Assizes begin *Rain*	3 13	6 39	5 20
22	frid	Dalhousie Assizes begin	4 27	6 41	5 18
23	sat	District Court Term ends	rises	6 42	5 17
24	A	[24 Bat Chateauguay 1813	5 53	6 44	5 16
25	mon	Colborne Assizes begin	6 40	6 45	5 14
26	tues	*Pleasant for*	7 31	6 47	5 13
27	wed	*the Season*	8 26	6 48	5 11
28	thur	Bathurst A b Simon & Jude	9 24	6 49	5 10
29	frid	Battle of Fort Erie 1812	10 23	6 51	5 9
30	sat		11 22	6 52	5 7
31	A	22nd Sunday after Trinity	morn	6 53	5 6

MOON'S CHANGES.

N *Moon* 7th, 10h 27m *eve* | F *Moon* 22nd, 5h 20m *mo*
First *Qr* 15th, 1h 31m *eve* | Last *Qr* 29th, 11h 38m *mo*

DM	D. W.	REMARKABLE DAYS, &c.	MOON rises	SUN rises	sets
1	mon	Michaelmas Term b All Saints	0 20	6 55	5 5
2	tues	All Souls. Insur L C 1838	1 18	6 56	5 4
3	wed	St Winifred *Cool*	2 15	6 57	5 2
4	thur	[5 Sir J Co'borne Lt G 1828	3 12	6 59	5 1
5	frid	Gunpowder Plot 1605	4 8	7 0	4 59
6	sat	Battle of Jemappes 1792	5 5	7 1	4 58
7	A	Battle of Tippecanoe 1811	se's	7 3	4 57
8	mon	Milton died 1674 *Look for*	5 22	7 4	4 56
9	tues	Battle of the Nivelle 1813	6 3	7 5	4 54
10	wed	[9 Prince of Wales b 1841	6 48	7 6	4 53
11	thur	Battle of Williamsburg 1813	7 39	7 8	4 52
12	frid	Leibnitz died 1716 *Rain*	8 35	7 9	4 51
13	sat	Michaelmas Term ends	9 35	7 10	4 50
14	A	24th Sunday after Trinity	10 39	7 11	4 48
15	mon	Battle of Arcole 1796	11 45	7 12	4 47
16	tues	Quarter Session & Dis Courts	morn	7 14	4 46
17	wed	Bat of Chrysler's Farm 1813	0 54	7 15	4 45
18	thur	Rubens b 1577 *Cold mornings*	2 5	7 16	4 44
19	frid	Jay's Treaty 1794	3 16	7 17	4 43
20	sat	[21 Princess Royal b 1840	4 30	7 18	4 42
21	A	25th Sunday after Trinity	5 42	7 19	4 41
22	mon	St Cecilia *and evenings*	rises	7 20	4 40
23	tues	Lieut Weir murdered 1837	6 8	7 21	4 39
24	wed	John Knox died 1572	7 6	7 22	4 38
25	thur	Battle of St Charles 1837	8 7	7 23	4 37
26	frid	Dr Watts died 1748 *Rain &*	9 8	7 24	4 36
27	sat	Lord Littleton d 1779 *perhaps*	10 8	7 25	4 35
28	A	Advent Sunday	11 8	7 25	4 34
29	mon	Goldsmith born 1731 *Snow*	morn	7 26	4 34
30	tues	St Andrew	0 6	7 27	4 33

MOON'S CHANGES.

N Moon 7th, 3h 47m *eve*	F Moon 21st, 5h 24m *eve*
First Qr 14th, 10h 42m *eve*	Last Qr 29th, 9h 4m *mo*

DM	D. W.	REMARKABLE DAYS, &c.	MOON rises	SUN rises	SUN sest
1	wed	Battle of Austerlitz 1805	1 3	7 28	4 32
2	thur	Bonaparte crowned 1804	2 0	7 29	4 31
3	frid	Battle of Hohenlinden 1800	2 57	7 29	4 31
4	sat	[5 Ney shot 1815	3 54	7 30	4 20
5	A	2nd Sunday in Advent	4 51	7 31	4 29
6	mon	District Court Term begins	5 49	7 31	4 29
7	tues	Gallows Hill Races 1837	sets	7 32	4 28
8	wed	[9 Battle of the Nive 1813	5 34	7 32	4 28
9	thur	Milton born 1608	6 28	7 33	4 27
10	frid	Louis XVI tried 1792	7 28	7 33	4 27
11	sat	District Court Term ends	8 31	7 34	4 26
12	A	3rd Sunday in Advent	9 37	7 34	4 26
13	mon	[12 Niagara burnt 1813	10 44	7 34	4 26
14	tues	Washington died 1799	11 53	7 35	4 25
15	wed	St Eustache destroyed 1837	morn	7 35	4 25
16	thur	Gt Fire in New York 1835	1 2	7 35	4 25
17	frid	[18 Sir H Davy b 1778	2 12	7 35	4 25
18	sat	Fort Nia taken 1813 *Frosty*	3 22	7 35	4 24
19	A	4th Sunday in Advent	4 32	7 36	4 24
20	mon	Gray born 1716 *and clear*	5 39	7 36	4 24
21	tues	St Thomas	rises	7 36	4 24
22	wed	Winter Solstice	5 48	7 36	4 24
23	thur	Newton born 1642	6 49	7 36	4 24
24	frid	Treaty of Ghent	7 51	7 36	4 24
25	sat	Christmas Day	8 52	7 36	4 24
26	A	St Stephen	9 52	7 35	4 25
27	mon	St John	10 51	7 35	4 25
28	tues	Innocents	11 48	7 35	4 25
29	wed	[28 Buffalo burnt 1813	morn	7 35	4 25
30	thur	*High wind*	0 45	7 34	4 26
31	frid	St Silvester *with snow*	1 42	7 34	4 26

THE LEGISLATION OF LAST SESSION.

Several important measures, affecting the interests of all classes of the inhabitants of Canada, were passed into law during the last session of Parliament; and these, as the most useful matter which can be presented in the pages of a work of extensive circulation, will be found annexed, either at length or in an abridged form.

THE DISTRICT COUNCIL ACT.

An Act to amend the laws relative to District Councils in Upper Canada.

(9th June, 1846.)

WHEREAS it is expedient to amend the Act hereinafter mentioned, establishing Municipal Authorities in and for the several Districts of Upper Canada: Be it therefore enacted by the Queen's Most Excellent Majesty, by and with the advice and consent of the Legislative Council and of the Legislative Assembly of the Province of Canada, constituted and assembled by virtue of and under the authority of an Act passed in the Parliament of the United Kingdom of Great Britain and Ireland, and intituled, "An Act to re-unite the Provinces of Upper and Lower Canada, and for the Government of Canada," and it is hereby enacted by the authority of the same, That for and notwithstanding anything to the contrary in the seventh section or in any other part of the Act passed in the Session held in the fourth and fifth years of Her Majesty's Reign, and intituled, "An Act to provide for the better internal Government of that part of this Province, which formerly constituted the Province of Upper Canada, by the establishment of Local or Municipal Authorities therein," the Township meetings for the election of Councillors to represent such Townships respectively, in the District Council, shall open and commence at ten of the clock in the forenoon of the day appointed for such meetings, and the Poll, (if a Poll be demanded) shall finally close at four of the clock in the afternoon of the same day.

B

2. And be it enacted, That for and notwithstanding as aforesaid, and in addition to the purposes for which the District Councils are by the thirty-ninth section of the said Act empowered to make By-laws, each District Council shall have power by a By-law or By-laws to be passed from time to time, to fix the site of a Town Hall and the place for holding the Township meetings in each or any Township in the District ; and all Township meetings authorized by law shall thereafter be held at the places so appointed, and not elsewhere.

3. And be it enacted, That for and notwithstanding any thing in the twelfth or in the fiftieth section or in any other part of the said Act, it shall be lawful for any District Council, in its discretion, by any By-law, to be passed for that purpose, to allow to each Member of such Council a sum not exceeding six shillings and three pence for each day he shall actually sit in Council, to be paid out of the District Funds in such manner and on such conditions as shall be directed in such By-law ; and such By-law may or may not, in the discretion of the Council, be made to apply to the meeting at which it shall be made, but shall not apply to more than four half-yearly meetings after that at which it shall be made, and to such duly authorized extraordinary meetings as shall be held before the last of the half-yearly meetings to which the By-law shall be made applicable, and which shall be therein clearly stated.

4. And be it enacted, That for and notwithstanding anything in the fourth section or in any other part of the said Act, the Warden appointed or to be appointed by the Governor for each District, shall go out of office from time to time when a Warden shall be appointed for such District under the provisions of this Act, and thereafter it shall not be lawful for the Governor of this Province to appoint any person to be Warden of such District.

5. And be it enacted, That at the first meeting of each District Council in any year, the Members of such Council shall and may, by a majority of the votes of the whole number of the Councillors present, elect some one of themselves to be the Warden of the District until his successor shall be elected

in like manner ; and at such election the Warden for the time
being shall preside, but shall not vote unless the votes be
equally divided, in which case he shall give a casting vote,
and may give such vote in his own favour if he be one of the
parties having an equal number of votes :   And the Warden
so elected shall remain Warden and shall preside at the
election of his successor although he may have gone out of
office as a Councillor before such election, but the Warden may
always be re-elected if he be a Councillor at the time of the
election : Provided always, that the Warden appointed for any
District by the Governor, shall, if otherwise qualified, be eligible as a Councillor at or after the annual election of Councillors, in the year one thousand eight hundred and forty-
seven.

6. And be it enacted, That the Warden so elected shall
while in office have all the powers and perform all the
duties assigned by the Act aforesaid to the Warden appointed
by the Governor, and the provisions of the said Act shall apply
to the Warden so elected and to all matters relating to his
office, in so far as may be consistent with this Act : And if at
any time a temporary Chairman shall be appointed under the
provisions of the twenty-first section of the said Act, during
the absence of the Warden, or in case of a vacancy in that
office, such temporary Chairman shall, during such absence
or vacancy, have all the powers and perform all the duties of
the Warden :   And if such vacancy or absence shall occur
during the interval between two Meetings, then the District
Clerk shall act as Warden, until a Warden or a temporary
Chairman shall be elected.

7. And be it enacted, That at the first meeting of District
or Municipal Councils after the passing of this Act, a District
Treasurer shall be selected by the majority of the votes of any
District or Municipal Council, any thing in the twenty-
ninth section of the before recited Act to the contrary notwithstanding, and shall be subject to re-election at the expiration
of every three years ; and such Treasurer so selected shall
have all rights and powers which by any enactments now in
force might appertain to any District Treasurer appointed before the passing hereof, in so far as the same may not be in-

consistent with the provisions of this Act; And at the expiration of three years as aforesaid, the Council, if they see fit for the public interests, may select any other person to discharge the duty of Treasurer other than the one first selected : And it is hereby provided, that on any vacancy in the office of District Treasurer by death or otherwise during the recess of the Council, the Warden may and shall summon an extra meeting of the Council, for the purpose of selecting a Treasurer as aforesaid.

8. And be it enacted, That any Treasurer selected by the provisions of this Act shall, before he enters on the duty of the said office, give security for the safe keeping and the lawful application of all monies which may come into his hands by virtue of any enactment of the Legislature of the late Province of Upper Canada, or of the Legislature of the Province of Canada, or of any By-laws of the Municipal or District Council : And such security shall be such Treasurer in the sum of Two Thousand Pounds, and two sufficient sureties to be approved of by the District Council, in the sum of One Thousand Pounds each.

9. And be it enacted, That for and notwithstanding any thing in the twenty-eighth section or in any other part of the said Act, the District Clerk appointed or to be appointed by the Governor in each District, shall go out of office from the time his successor shall be appointed under this Act, and thereafter no District Clerk shall be appointed by the Governor in such District.

10. And be it enacted, That at their first meeting in the year One Thousand Eight Hundred and Forty-seven, each District Council shall appoint a proper person to be the District Clerk, and may from time to time remove him, and appoint another in his stead, or may replace him; and the District Clerk so appointed shall have all the powers and perform all the duties assigned to the District Clerk by the Act aforesaid, and shall be subject to all the provisions thereof in so far as may be consistent with this Act; Provided always, that the Clerk of the Peace for the District shall always be eligible as District Clerk; and that in case of any vacancy occurring in the office of District Clerk during the interval be-

tween two meetings of the Council, the Clerk of the Peace for the District shall be *ex officio* the District Clerk until another shall be appointed as aforesaid.

11. And be it enacted, That for and notwithstanding any thing in the twenty-second section or in any other part of the said Act, there shall only be two ordinary meetings of each District Council in each year, which shall be held in the months of February and October, in each year; and the said half-yearly meetings shall commence on the first Tuesday in each of the months of February and October, respectively, and shall not be held for a longer period than nine successive days, (Sundays excepted;) and all the provisions of the said Act as to the quarterly meetings therein mentioned shall apply to the half-yearly meetings appointed by this Act or by any By-law made under the authority thereof, in so far as may be consistent with this Act; and any thing which, by the said Act or by the By-laws of any District Council, shall have been appointed to be done at the quarterly meeting which without this Act would have been held in the month of August or of November, shall and may be done at the half-yearly meeting to be held in the month of October of the same year.

12. Provided always, And be it enacted, That any District Council may, by By-laws to be from time to time made in that behalf, and expressly approved by the Governor in Council, alter the period hereinbefore fixed for the ordinary half-yearly meetings of such District Council and the duration of such meetings, so that no more than two such meetings be appointed to be held in any year, and that no such meeting be held for a longer period than nine successive days, Sundays and Good Friday excepted.

13. And be it enacted, That the forty-second section of the Act of the Legislature of Upper Canada, passed in the first year of Her Majesty's Reign and intituled "An Act to alter and amend sundry Acts, regulating the appointment and duties of Township Officers," and so much of the twenty-third section of the said Act as enables any party to compound for Statute labor, or fixes the rate of composition, or the officer to whom the composition money shall be paid, or the manner in which it shall be employed, shall be repealed; and that for and not-

withstanding anything in the Act first above cited and hereby amended, it shall be lawful for the District Council by any By-law, to empower the landholders in the District to compound for the Statute labor by them respectively performable, for any term not exceeding five years at any rate not exceeding two shillings and six pence for each day's labor, and at any time before the labor compounded for ought to be performed, and by such By-law to direct to what officer in each Township such composition money shall be paid, and how such money shall be applied and accounted for, and to regulate by By-law the manner and the divisions in which the Statute labor shall be performed, or to empower the respective Township Councillors to direct the laying out and performance thereof.

14. And be it enacted, That in addition to the purposes for which the District Councils are empowered by the Act first above cited to make By-laws, it shall be lawful for any District Council to make By-laws for providing that on each side of any highway which shall pass through a wood, the timber shall be cut down for a space not exceeding twenty-five feet on each side of such highway, by the proprietor of the land on which such timber shall be, or in his default by the Overseer of Highways in whose division such land shall lie ; such timber to be removed by the proprietor within a time to be appointed by the By-law, or in his default by such Overseer of Roads, in which last mentioned case it may be used by the Overseer for any purpose connected with the improvement of the highways and bridges in his division, or sold by him to defray the expenses incurred in carrying the By-law into effect : Provided always, that no such By-law shall authorize or compel the cutting down of any orchard or shrubbery, or of any trees planted expressly for ornament or shelter.

15. And be it enacted, That for and notwithstanding anything in the thirty-seventh or in the forty-sixth section, or in any part of the Act first above cited, it shall be discretionary with each District Council to employ the District Surveyor to prepare, examine or report upon the estimate for any work upon which the sum to be expended shall not exceed fifty pounds, or for any other purpose relative to such work.

16. And be it enacted, That in addition to the purposes for

which the District Councils are empowered by the forty-eighth section of the Act first above cited to make By-laws, it shall be lawful for any District Council, on the application of a majority of the persons qualified to vote at the election of Township officers in any Township in the District, to authorize and direct by By-law, the raising by assessment on the taxable property in such Township, of such sum as may be required for the purpose of affording relief to indigent, sick or infirm persons in the Township, in such manner and under such regulations as may be provided in any By-law to be made in that behalf.

17. And be it enacted, That all the provisions of the forty-seventh section of the Act first above cited, and all other provisions of the said Act, shall apply to the By-laws to be made and other proceedings to be had under this Act, in so far as may be consistent with this Act.

18. And be it enacted, That for and notwithstanding any thing in the eleventh section of the said recited Act, it shall and may be lawful for the inhabitants of any Township or reputed Township to elect any person or persons to be a District Councillor or Councillors, although such person or persons may not be resident within the Township or reputed Township for which he or they may be elected.

19. And be it enacted, That for and notwithstanding any thing in the thirty-seventh section of the said first recited Act, the District Surveyor, appointed by the Warden of any District, shall go out of office from the time his successor shall be appointed under this Act, and thereafter no District Surveyor shall be appointed by the Warden of any District: Provided always, that any present District Surveyor may be appointed to perform the duties of that office by the District Council.

20. And be it enacted, That at their first meeting, in the year one thousand eight hundred and forty-seven, the District Council shall appoint a proper person to be District Surveyor, and may from time to time remove him and appoint another in his stead, or may replace him; and the District Surveyor so appointed shall have all the powers and perform all the duties assigned to the said District Surveyor by the

Act aforesaid, and shall be subject to all the provisions thereof, in so far as may be consistent with this Act.

21. And be it enacted, That this Act shall come into effect upon, from and after the third Monday in August next, and shall apply solely to that part of this Province which formerly constituted the Province of Upper Canada.

22. And be it enacted, That the word "Governor," wherever it occurs in this Act, shall be construed as including the Lieutenant-Governor or Person administering the Government of this Province; and that the words "Governor in Council" shall be construed as meaning the Governor acting by and with the advice of the Executive Council of this Province.

THE SCHOOL ACT.

The "*Act for the better establishment and maintenance of Common Schools in Upper Canada,*" provides as follows:—

That the Governor may, from time to time, by Letters Patent, under the Great Seal of the Province, appoint a fit and proper person to be Superintendent of Schools, in Upper Canada, and to hold his office during pleasure; that the said Superintendent shall receive a Salary not to exceed five hundred pounds, currency, per annum, and to bear such proportion to that sum as the amount of public moneys paid towards the support of Common Schools in that part of this Province called Upper Canada, bears to that paid towards the support of Common Schools in that part of this Province called Lower Canada, and shall be allowed one hundred and seventy-five pounds, currency, per annum, for a Clerk, and the contingent expenses of his office, to be by him accounted for, as provided in respect of other public officers; and that the said Superintendent shall be subject to all such lawful orders and directions, in the exercise of his duties, as shall from time to time be given by the Governor of this Province.

2. That it shall be the duty of the Superintendent of Schools;

First, After deducting certain sums as hereinafter provided, to apportion, on or before the fifteenth day of April of each year, all moneys appropriated by the Legislature for Common Schools in Upper Canada for such year, according to the ratio of population in each District, Township or City, as compared with the population of Upper Canada, or if he shall think it expedient, in case of a defective Census, according to the ratio of children residing in each, over the age of five and under the age of sixteen years, as stated in the last Annual Reports of the District Superintendents.

Secondly, To certify such apportionment made by him to the Inspector General, so far as it relates to the several Districts in Upper Canada ; also to give immediate notice to the Superintendent of Schools in each District, stating the amount of moneys appropriated to his District, and to each Township, Town and City therein.

Thirdly, To prepare suitable forms and regulations for making all Reports, and conducting all necessary proceedings under this Act, and to cause the same, with such instructions as he shall deem necessary and proper for the better organization and government of Common Schools, to be transmitted to the Officers required to execute the provisions of this Act, copies of which forms, regulations and instructions, as also copies of this Act shall be furnished by him to the several District Superintendents, for the use of School sections, as occasion may require.

Fourthly, To see that all moneys apportioned by him be applied to the purposes for which they were granted.

Fifthly, To decide upon all matters and complaints which may be submitted to him by parties interested, under the operation of this Act.

Sixthly, To discourage the use of unsuitable and improper books in the Schools or School Libraries, and to use all lawful means to provide for and recommend the use of uniform and approved text books in all the Schools.

Seventhly, To take the general superintendence of the Normal School, as soon as one shall have been established.

Eighthly, To prepare, as soon as practicable, and recommend the adoption of suitable plans of School Houses, with the proper furniture and appendages.

Ninthly, To use his best endeavours to promote the establishment of School Libraries for general reading in the several Districts and Townships of Upper Canada, and to furnish every information necessary, as far as he shall be able, as to the regulations of such institutions and the books most suitable for them.

Tenthly, To employ all lawful means in his power to collect and diffuse information on the subject of education generally, among the people of Upper Canada.

Eleventhly, To submit annually to the Governor of this Province, on or before the first day of August in each year, a report of the actual state of the Normal, Model and Common Schools throughout Upper Canada, shewing the amount of moneys expended on such Schools, and from what sources the same have been derived, with plans for their improvement, and such other statements and suggestions relating to education generally as the said Superintendent may deem useful and expedient, in order that the same may be laid before the Legisgislature.

3. That the Governor shall have authority to appoint not more than seven persons, (of whom the Superintendent of Schools shall be one, to be a Board of Education,) who shall hold their situation during pleasure, and shall be subject to all lawful orders and directions in the exercise of their duties which shall from time to time be issued by the Governor, and whose duty it shall be, in conjunction with the Superintendent of Schools—

First, To adopt all needful measures for the establishment and furnishing of a Normal School for Upper Canada,—to make from time to time all needful rules and regulations for the management and good government of such School—to prescribe the conditions on which pupils shall be received and instructed therein,—to select the location of such School, the terms and conditions on which buildings therefor shall be procured,—to determine the number and compensation of Teachers and others who may be employed therein,—and to do all other lawful things which they may deem expedient to promote the objects and interests of such School.

Secondly, To examine and recommend or disapprove of all

books, plans or forms which may be submitted to them with a view to their use in Schools : and no portion of the Government Grant shall be given in aid of any School in which any book is used which has been disapproved of by the Board, and of which disapproval public notice shall have been given.

Thirdly, To aid the Superintendent of Schools with their counsel and advice on all questions, and on all measures which he may submit to them for the promotion of the interests of Schools and for the diffusion of useful knowledge among the people of Upper Canada.

4. That the meetings of the said Board shall be held at some place which shall be provided by the Superintendent of Schools ; and that the first meeting of the Board shall be called by the Superintendent of Schools ; that the said Board shall appoint a Chairman, and the times of its meetings ; that a special meeting may be called at any time by the Superintendent of Schools, by giving due notice to the other members ; that at all meetings of the Board duly called, three members shall form a *quorum* for the transaction of business ; that the Clerk in the Education Office shall be the Recording Clerk to the Board ; and shall enter all its proceedings in a book to be kept for that purpose ; and that the expenses attending the proceedings of the Board shall be accounted for as part of the contingent expenses of the Education Office.

5. That as soon as practicable, there shall be established a *Normal School*, containing one or more elementary *Model Schools* for the instruction and practice of Teachers of Common Schools in the science of education and art of teaching, according to such regulations as are hereinbefore provided for, and which shall be approved by the Governor in Council, and that a sum not exceeding one thousand five hundred pounds, be expended by the Board of Education in procuring and furnishing suitable buildings for the said Normal School ; and that a sum not exceeding one thousand five hundred pounds per annum be allowed for the salaries of Teachers and all other contingent expenses of the said School ; and that detailed accounts of the expenditure of all moneys for

the establishment and support of the said School shall be annually transmitted to the Governor, through the Superintendent of Schools, to be laid before the Legislature.

6. That the Council of each District shall have authority to appoint a proper person to be District Superintendent of Common Schools who shall hold his office during pleasure: Provided always, that in case the Council of any District shall neglect or refuse to recommend the appointment of a District Superintendent at any meeting of such Council during the present year, or at their first meeting after the occurrence of any vacancy, then it shall be lawful for the Governor to make such appointment.

7. That it shall be lawful for the Council of each District, by By-law, to provide for the salary of the District Superintendent.

8. That the Council of each District, on receiving from the District Superintendent of Common Schools, a certified copy of the apportionment of the Legislative Grant in aid of Common Schools in their District for the current year, shall, without delay, cause to be levied such sum of money, for Common School purposes, as they shall see fit, and within the limit of their power for imposing taxes, and at least equal (clear of all charges of collection) to the amount of public moneys apportioned to such District, such sum, within the limit aforesaid, to be increased at the discretion of the said Council; and the sum so to be raised shall be placed on the proper Collector's Rolls, and shall be collected by him in like manner as any other tax for such District, but shall be paid over by him to the District Superintendent of Common Schools, within the period fixed by law for the payment of rates collected to the Treasurer in each year.

9. That the Council of each District shall cause each Township, or parts of adjoining Townships, Town or City in such District, to be divided into a convenient number of sections and parts of sections to be numbered and described; and which may be altered at the discretion of the Council; and a copy of the descriptions and numbers of such sections and parts of sections shall be forthwith furnished by the Clerk of such Council to the Superintendent of Common Schools for the District.

10. That the District Council in each District shall have authority within the limit aforesaid, to cause to be levied any sum or sums of money which may be required for the purchasing of School sites, and the erection and furnishing of School Houses, the procuring of residences for Teachers, and for Common School purposes generally, in such District, and upon the inhabitants of the said District generally, or on those of any particular Township, School section, or other locality, as the case may require ; Provided always, that this shall not be construed to prevent the inhabitants of any School section or Township from adopting any voluntary means they may deem expedient to purchase, erect, furnish, or repair any School House or residence for the Teacher : Provided always, that the title to any Common School House and the land and premises appurtenant thereto, now vested in Trustees or other persons, to and for the use of any Common School, or hereafter to be purchased, acquired and conveyed for such use, shall be vested in the District Council of the District in which such School Houses and lands are situate, in trust for the use of such Schools, respectively.

11. That where, under or by virtue of any Act of the Legislature of this Province for the establishment or maintenance of Common Schools, any School House shall have been erected which, from any cause whatever, shall not have been paid for to the person or persons entitled to the same, and for which a rate shall not have been assessed upon the School section, (or where such rate shall have been imposed but has not been collected) in which the same was so built, it shall and may be lawful to and for the District Council of the District in which the same is situate, to levy by assessment, a rate upon the inhabitants of such School section sufficient in amount to pay the same.

12. That each District Superintendent, appointed as hereinbefore provided, shall, before he enters upon the duties of his office, enter into bonds with two or more sufficient sureties, to such an amount and in such form as may be required by the Council of the District, for the faithful performance of the duties of his office.

13. That it shall be the duty of each District Superintendent of Common Schools :

First, To transmit to the Clerk of the District Council, to be laid before the Council, a certified copy of the apportionment of School money to be distributed in the District, as soon as the notice of the said apportionment shall have been received from the Superintendent of Schools.

Secondly, As soon as he shall receive from the District Clerk a notification of the amount of money required by the District Council to be raised by tax, to add that amount to the Government apportionment, (which two sums added together shall constitute the District School Fund for the support of Common Schools in such District,) and to apportion the said fund among the several School sections entitled to receive the same, according to the ratio of children over five and under sixteen years of age in such sections respectively, as compared with the whole number of children of the same ages in each Township, Town, or City, and in the whole District, and to notify the same to the Trustees of each School section in the District, so far as they are respectively concerned.

Thirdly, To pay to any Teacher or his agent, on any order or orders of the Trustees for the time being or the majority of them, as hereinafter provided, any sum or sums of money which have been apportioned to the School or School section in which such Teacher may have taught ; the payment of which order shall nevertheless be subject to the following conditions :

He shall not pay any parts of the apportionment to any School section from which no sufficient Annual Report shall have been received for the year ending the last day of December preceding the apportionment.

Nor shall he pay any part of the apportionment to any School section, or part of a section, unless it shall appear by the said Reports that a School has been kept therein for at least six months during the year ending at the date of such Report, by a qualified Teacher, and that all moneys received from the School Fund during the year ending at the date of such Report, have been faithfully applied in paying the compensation of such Teacher : Provided likewise, that the foregoing condition shall not be exacted of a School section in which a School has been commenced during the preceding year,—such newly formed section being entitled to share in the School Fund, provided a School shall have been kept therein three months in the year preceding by a qualified Teacher, and a sufficient Report furnished.

Fourthly, To visit all the Model and Common Schools in his District, at least once a year, and oftener if it be deemed necessary, in order to examine into the state and condition of the Schools, both as respects the progress of the scholars in learning, and the good order of the Schools, and the character and condition of the buildings, and to give such advice both to Teachers and Trustees, in regard to the interests and management of the Schools, as he may judge proper.

Fifthly, To examine all persons offering themselves as Candidates for teaching in Common Schools, with respect to their moral character, learning and ability ; and if he be satisfied of the Candidate's qualifications in these respects. he shall give him a special certificate, authorizing him to teach only one year in the School specified, or a general certificate authorizing the applicant to teach in any Common School in the District until such Certificate is revoked : Provided always, that every such Teacher shall be subject to re-examination whenever it shall be deemed expedient, by the District Superintendent of Schools : Provided also, that no such Certificate of qualification shall be granted to any person as a Teacher, who shall not at the time of granting it, be a natural born or naturalized subject of Her Majesty, Her Heirs or Successors, without a special license in the case of a Teacher of any language other than English, to be obtained from the Governor, authorizing the person therein named to be employed as a Teacher although an alien.

Sixthly, To annul any Certificate given by him or any of his predecessors in office, whenever he shall see just cause for doing so, assigning his reasons, and giving the Teacher holding such Certificate, an opportunity if he shall feel himself aggrieved, to appeal to the Superintendent of Schools.

Seventhly, To prevent the use of all unauthorized foreign school books in the English branches of education, to recommend the use of proper books for Schools, and to determine as to the Teacher, and regulations of Model Schools, in the manner hereinafter provided.

Eighthly, To decide upon all questions of dispute which may arise between any of the parties interested under the operation of this Act, and which may be submitted to him by either of the parties concerned : Provided always, that he may, if he shall deem it advisable, refer any such question as may be submitted to him to the Superintendent of Schools ; Provided also, that any aggrieved or dissatisfied party shall have the right of appeal to the Superintendent of Schools.

Ninthly, To retain in his hands, subject to the order of the Superintendent of Schools, all moneys which may have been apportioned for his District for the year, and which have not been called for or expended according to the provisions of this Act.

Tenthly, To act in accordance with the directions of the Superintendent of Schools, and to make an Annual Report to him, at such time and in such form as may be appointed by the said Superintendent of Schools; and to furnish the said Superintendent from time to time with such additional information as he may require : Provided furthermore. that every such Annual Report of the District Superintendent shall state :

First, The whole number of School sections or parts of sections separately set off within each Township, Town or City in his District.

Secondly, The number of children taught in each of the said sections or parts of sections over the age of five and under the age of sixteen years ; and also the number of children residing in each, over the age of five and under sixteen years.

Thirdly, The length of time a School shall have been kept in each of such sections or parts of sections, by a qualified Teacher, the books used and the subjects taught, and whether the Trustees have duly reported.

Fourthly, The amount of moneys which have been received by and collected in each of the said sections and parts of sections—distinguishing the amount apportioned by the Superintendent of Schools, the amount received from the District School Tax, the amounts raised by the Trustees, and the amount from any other and what sources ; also how all such moneys have been expended, and whether any and what part remains unexpended, and from what cause or causes.

Fifthly, The number of his School visits during the year, the whole number of School Houses in each Township, Town or City, the number hired, and the number erected during the year, and of what character and by what means.

Sixthly, So far as he may be able to ascertain, the number of private Schools kept in each Township, Town or City in his District, the number of the pupils and the subjects taught therein.

Seventhly, The number and extent of the School and public Libraries in his District, where situate, how established and supported ; also any other information which he may possess respecting the educational state, wants, and advantages of his District, and any suggestions he may think proper to make with a view to the improvement of the Schools and the diffusion of useful knowledge in such District.

14. And be it enacted, That the Visitors of each Township, Town or City, shall be—all Clergymen or Ministers recognized by law, of whatever denomination, who reside or have pastoral charge in such Township, Town or City, the Judge of the District Court, the Warden of the District, and the Councillor or Councillors representing the Township in the Municipal Council of the District,—also all resident Justices of the Peace—but no Minister, Priest, Ecclesiastic, or Justice of the Peace shall be entitled to visit or inspect any *separate* School not of his own persuasion, except by the consent of the Trustees of such School.

15. And be it enacted, That it shall be lawful for each of the said Visitors, to visit as far as practicable all the Schools in such Township, Town or City,—especially to attend the quarterly examinations of Schools, and at the time of such visit to examine the progress of the pupils, and the state and management of the School, and to give such advice to the Teacher and pupils as he may deem expedient according to the regula-

C

tions and directions for Visitors which shall be prepared by the Superintendent of Schools : It shall also be lawful for such Visitors as may be present at any School Examination to report the same with any remarks they may think proper, to the District Superintendent, and to make either collectively or individually to the said District Superintendent such other Report or Reports as they may judge expedient, respecting the condition, character and progress of the Schools in such Township, Town or City.

16. And be it enacted, That a General Meeting of such Visitors may be held at any time or place which may be appointed by the Senior Justice of the Peace, or any two Visitors, on sufficient notice being given to the other Visitors in such Township, Town or City, and that it may be lawful for such Visitors thus assembled, to devise such means as they may deem expedient for the efficient visitation of the Common Schools, and to promote the establishment of Libraries and the diffusion of useful knowledge in such Township, Town or City ; it shall also be lawful for any two of such Visitors to examine and give a Certificate in a form prescribed by the Superintendent of Schools, to any Candidate for teaching whom they shall judge qualified to teach in a Common School: such Certificate, however, only authorizing the applicant to teach one year in the School specified.

17. And be it enacted, That whenever any School section shall be formed in any Township, Town or City, it shall be the duty of the municipal authority to designate some person or persons in such section, to whom the District Superintendent shall communicate the description and number of such section, and which person or persons shall, within twenty days thereafter prepare a notice in writing, describing such section, and appointing a time and place for the first School section meeting, and shall cause copies of such notice to be posted in at least three public places in such School section, at least six days before the time of holding such meeting.

18. And be it enacted, That after such first School section meeting there shall be a like meeting held in such School section on the second Tuesday of January in each year, at the

hour of twelve of the clock at noon, at such place as shall be specified by a majority of the School Trustees in such section, who shall cause notices of such Annual Meeting to be posted in at least three public places in such School section, at least six days before the time of holding such meeting.

19. And be it enacted, That at every such first School section meeting, and at every such Annual School section meeting, the Senior Justice of the Peace present, or in default of any Justice of the peace being present, such other person as shall be appointed by a majority of the landholders and householders of such School section who shall be present at such meeting, shall preside over the proceedings of such meeting, and shall, immediately after such meeting, communicate to the District Superintendent the name or names and address of the person or persons chosen Trustee or Trustees, and the number of their School section.

20. And be it enacted, That should no such first or Annual School section meeting be held in consequence of the notice hereinbefore required not having been given, the person or persons whose duty it was to give such notice shall individually forfeit a sum not exceeding two pounds, which shall be recoverable for the School purposes of such section, by prosecution before any Justice of the Peace, who is hereby authorized on the complaint on oath of any two inhabitants of such section to hear and determine the same and to convict the party and to issue a warrant to levy the penalty by such sale and distress of the offender's goods :—And in such default of holding such meeting, any three resident freeholders shall have authority within twenty days after the time at which such meeting should have been held, to call such meeting by giving six days notice, to be posted in at least three public places in such School section.

21. And be it enacted, That at the first School section meeting which shall be held in a newly formed section, the landholders and householders thereat shall elect three Trustees, who shall continue in Office until the next ensuing Annual School meeting of such section.

22. And be it enacted, That at the first Annual School meeting held in any School section after the passing of this Act, the persons qualified to vote thereat shall elect, by a majority of votes, three Trustees who shall be numbered one, two, three ; (the order to be determined by lot,) the first of whom shall continue in office one year, the second two years, the third three years, at the end of which periods they shall respectively be replaced by others ; and that at each succeeding Annual School meeting of such section, the persons present qualified to vote shall elect one Trustee, who shall continue in office three years, until a successor is elected ; provided that any Trustee, if willing, may be re-elected.

23. And be it enacted, That if any person chosen as a Trustee shall refuse to serve, he shall forfeit a sum not exceeding five pounds, which sum shall be collected and applied in the same manner as other fines imposed by this Act ; and if one or more vacancies shall occur among the Trustees, by reason of refusal to serve, permanent absence from the School section, death or incapacity from sickness, such vacancy or vacancies shall be filled up by the electors of such School section at a meeting to be called for that purpose by the surviving Trustee or Trustees ; and in case of there being no surviving Trustee, the District Council of the District shall fill up the vacancies, and the person or persons who shall be appointed to fill up a vacancy or vacancies shall continue in office during the period for which the person or persons whom he or they shall succeed would have been required to serve.

24. And be it enacted, That no School Trustee shall be re-elected except by his own consent during the four years next after his going out of office.

25. And be it enacted, That the School Trustees in each School section, shall be a Corporation, under the name of "*The* "*School Trustees of Section number*   *in the Township, (Town or City,) of*   *in the* "   *District.*"—and shall have perpetual succession, and a common Seal, and may sue and be sued, and shall generally have the same powers which any other body politic or corporate has with regard to the purposes for

which it is constituted ; but they shall not at any time hold real property.

26. And be it enacted, That no such Corporation shall cease by reason of the want of School Trustees, but in such case the powers of the Corporation as regards the possession of any personal property shall become vested in the District Superintendent, in trust, until it shall be otherwise provided by law, and the School House, lands or other real property, belonging to the Common School or Common Schools, in any section under any law or by any title whatsoever, is hereby vested in the District Council, for the several Common Schools and in trust for such Schools respectively.

27. And be it enacted, That it shall be the duty of the Trustees of each School section :

First, To appoint one of themselves Secretary-Treasurer, who shall keep a Minute of their proceedings in a book kept for that purpose,—shall receive the moneys collected by rate bill or subscription from the inhabitants of the School section, —and shall be responsible for such moneys to his colleagues, and shall pay them to the Teacher after defraying the expense of collection, in such manner as may be directed by the majority of the Trustees.

Secondly, To appoint a Collector if they shall think it expedient, to collect the sums which they have imposed upon the inhabitants of their School section, or which the said inhabitants may have subscribed, and to pay such Collector not to exceed at the rate of five per cent. for his trouble in collecting ; and every Collector shall give such security as may be satisfactory to the Trustees, and shall have the same power in collecting the School rate, or subscription, and proceed in the same manner and be subject to the same liabilities in the discharge of his duty as is or may be by law provided in respect of Collectors of the district rates and assessments.

Thirdly, To take possession of all Common School property, which may have been acquired or given for Common School purposes in such section, and to acquire and hold for the Corporation by any title whatsoever, all personal property, moneys or income for Common School purposes, until the power hereby given shall be taken away or modified by law, and to apply the same according to the terms of acquiring or receiving them.

Fourthly, To do whatever may be expedient with regard to building, repairing, renting, renewing, warming or keeping in order the School House and its appendages, lands, fences and moveable property which shall be held by them : Provided that no rate shall be levied for the building of a School House in any School section otherwise than under a By-Law of the District Council, but such By-law may be made by the District Council at any meeting thereof, and the rate may be forthwith placed on the Collector's Rolls by the Clerk of the Peace, and collected by the Collector ; any thing in any Act passed during the present Session, or at any previous time, and limiting the period at which By-Laws, imposing taxes, are to be passed in any year to the contrary notwithstanding.

Fifthly, To cause in their discretion to be levied by rate bill, in the manner hereinafter provided by this Act, or by voluntary subscriptions any additional sum that may be necessary to pay the salary of the Teacher and the incidental expenses of the School, such as repairing, furnishing and keeping the School House in order, and in case there be no School House, providing a suitable place for the School, providing fuel in a state fit for use in the School House selected, and all things necessary for the comfort of the pupils ; and before such Trustees, or any one on their behalf shall be entitled to receive from the District Superintendent their share of the Common School Fund, they shall furnish him with a declaration from the Secretary-Treasurer, that he has actually and *bona fide* received and has in his possession for the payment of the Teacher, or has paid such Teacher a sum sufficient with such allowance from the Common School fund for the purposes aforesaid.

Sixthly, To prepare and determine a rate bill quarterly, containing the name of every person liable to pay for the instruction of children sent by him to such Schools, and the amount for which he is liable, and by themselves or any one of them, or by their Collector, to collect from every person named in such rate bill the amount therein charged against him, and in case they employ a Collector, five *per centum* on such amount for the cost of collection, and to pay the amount so collected to the Teacher or Teachers entitled to receive the same ; Provided that every person sending a child or children to any Common School, shall be rated for a period of not less than two-thirds of the current quarter.

Seventhly, To exempt wholly or in part from the payment of the rate bill such indigent persons within their School section as they shall think proper ; and in default of payment by any person rated, to levy the amount by distress, and sale of the goods and chattels of the person or persons making default ; and in case such person or persons reside without the School section, and have no goods or chattels within it, at the time of making such collection, to sue and recover by their name of office, the amount from such person or persons ; and for the collection of such rate, the Collector appointed by the Trustees shall have, within their School section, the same powers as the Collector of any District rates.

Eighthly, To ascertain the number of children residing in their School section, over the age of five and under sixteen years, and to allow them, without exception, to attend the Common School, so long as their conduct shall be agreeable to the rules of such School.

Ninthly, To appoint and engage, from time to time, a Teacher duly qualified to teach in the School under their control, according to the provisions of this Act ; and to give such Teacher the necessary orders upon the District Superintendent for the portion of the School Fund, to which their School section may be entitled.

Tenthly, To select from a list of books, made out by the Board of Education, under the sanction of the Governor in Council, as hereinbefore provided, the books which shall be used in the School.

Eleventhly To see that the School is conducted according to the regulations herein provided for ; and to prepare and transmit annually on or before the second Tuesday in January, a Report to the District Superintendent, which Report shall be signed by a majority of the Trustees, and made according to a form which shall be provided by the Superintendent of Schools, and shall specify :

1st, The whole time a School has been kept by a qualified Teacher or Teachers in their section during the year ending the thirty-first day of the previous December, the day before that on which the Report shall be dated, except when the year commences on a Sunday, in which case the Report shall be dated on the second day of January in the year in which it shall be transmitted.

2ndly, The amount of moneys received from the District Superintendent, and the amount of moneys received from other sources, distinguishing the same ; and the manner in which all such moneys have been expended.

3rdly, The number of children taught in the section School during the year, and the number of children residing in the section, over the age of five years and under the age of sixteen.

4thly, The branches taught in the School ; the number of pupils in each ; and the text books used.

28. And be it enacted, That it shall be the duty of every Teacher of a Common School—

First, To teach, diligently and faithfully, all the branches required to be taught in the School, according to the terms of his engagement with the Trustees, and according to the provisions of this Act.

Secondly, To keep the daily, weekly and quarterly registers of the School, and to maintain proper order and discipline therein, according to the regulations and forms which shall be prepared by the Superintendent of Schools.

Thirdly, To have, at the end of each quarter, a public examination of his School, of which he shall give notice ,through the children, to their parents and guardians, and shall also give due notice to the Trustees and any School Visitors who may reside in or adjacent to such School section.

Fourthly, To act as the Secretary to the Trustees, if they shall require it, in preparing their Annual Report : Provided always, that he is a Teacher in such School at the time of preparing such Report as is required by this Act : Provided likewise, that the District Superintendent shall have authority to withhold from any School section the remainder of the share of the Common School Fund which has been apportioned to such section, and which shall be in his hands on the first day of December of each year, until he receives from the Trustees of such section their Annual Report required by law for such year.

29. And be it enacted, That the sum of money annually distributed for the encouragement of Common Schools in Upper Canada, shall be payable on the first day of August in each year, by warrants to the Superintendents of Common Schools of the several Districts in Upper Canada aforesaid.

30. And be it enacted, That no foreign books in the English branches of education shall be used in any Model or Common School, except by the express permission of the Board of Education.

31. And be it enacted, That in any Model or Common School established under this Act, no child shall be required to read or study in or from any religious book, or to join in any exercise of devotion or religion which shall be objected to by his or her parents or guardians.

32. And be it enacted, That in all cases wherein the Teacher of any Common School shall happen to be a Roman Catholic, the Protestant inhabitants of the section to which such School belongs shall be entitled to have a School with a Protestant Teacher, upon the application of ten or more resident landholders or householders of any such School section, or within the limits assigned to any Town or City School; and in like manner when the Teacher of any such School shall happen to be a Protestant, the Roman Catholic inhabitants shall have a separate School, with a Teacher of their own religious persuasion, upon a like application.

33. And be it enacted, That such applications shall be made in writing, signed with the name of each landholder or householder, and addressed and transmitted to the District Superintendent; and such application shall contain the names of three Trustees who shall be the Trustees of such separate School; and upon the compliance of such Trustees

with the requirements of this Act, such School shall be entitled to receive its share of the public appropriation, according to the number of children of the religious class or persuasion who shall attend such separate School : which share shall be determined by the District Superintendent ; and such separate School shall be subject to the visitations, conditions, rules and obligations provided in this Act, with reference to other Common Schools.

34.   And be it enacted, That it shall be lawful for the Council of any District in Upper Canada, if they deem it proper to do so, to raise and levy by District rate, a sum not exceeding in any one year two hundred pounds, and to appropriate and expend the same for the maintenance of one or more District Model Schools within such District, appointing at least three Trustees of each such Model School ; Provided always, that by such By-law or By-laws there shall be appropriated from the District rates for the payment of Teachers and the purchase of books and apparatus and other necessary expenses for each Model School, a sum of not less than forty pounds yearly.

35.   And be it enacted, That whenever it shall appear to the satisfaction of the Governor, that any such District Council has thus appropriated and expended in any year for the payment of a Teacher or Teachers, and the purchase of books and apparatus for such District Model School or Schools, a sum not less than forty pounds, it shall be lawful for the Governor to issue his Warrant to the Receiver General, directing him to pay to the District Superintendent of such District, as a further aid towards the support of such School or Schools during such year, a sum equal to one half of the amount so raised and expended ; Provided always, that there be not thus granted in any year, for the support of such Schools in any one District, a larger sum than fifty pounds, and also that the whole amount thus to be granted in any one year, for the support of District Model Schools in Upper Canada, do not exceed five hundred pounds.

36. And be it enacted, That the Superintendent of Schools, before making the yearly apportionment of the grant in aid of Common Schools as hereinbefore provided, shall deduct from the same the aggregate of all amounts thus advanced for the support of the Normal Schools and District Model Schools during the preceding year; and he shall also deduct, if he shall deem it expedient, a sum not exceeding two hundred pounds per annum, in aid of Common Schools in new Townships not yet represented in any District Council.

37. And be it enacted, That all moneys to be thus granted in aid of District Model Schools, shall be expended by the District Superintendent receiving the same, or by his successor in office, in the payment of Teachers and the purchase of books and apparatus and other necessary expenses for such Schools exclusively, and within the year for which the same shall have been granted, and he shall account for the expenditure or non-expenditure of such moneys in the same manner as he is required to account for all other School moneys which may come into his hands.

38. And be it enacted, That it shall not be competent for the Trustees of any District Model School constituted as aforesaid, to appoint any person to be Teacher in the same, unless with a special approval in writing by the District Superintendent of their selection of such person as a Teacher, and also of the terms of their engagement with him; nor yet to make any arrangement for the internal administration of such School, unless in like manner approved by the District Superintendent; and the said District Superintendent shall have power to suspend or dismiss any such Teacher if he shall consider it necessary to do so, and to appoint any person to be a Teacher to any vacancy which the Trustees may refuse or neglect to fill up within thirty days after he shall have notified them of the same; and also, to make and enforce any regulations he may see fit to make for the administration of such Schools.

39. And be it enacted, That whenever a Normal School shall be in operation in Upper Canada, no person shall be

appointed to be a principal Teacher in any District Model School, who shall not have produced to the District Superintendent a Certificate of qualification and ability, signed by the principal or Head Master of such Normal School.

40. And be it enacted, That at every such District Model School, gratuitous instruction shall be afforded to all Teachers of Common Schools within the District in which such Model School may be established, during such period and under such regulations as the District Superintendent may from time to time direct.

41. And be it enacted, That the Teachers who shall receive Certificates of qualification under this Act shall be arranged in three classes, according to their attainments and ability, in such manner as shall be prescribed by the Superintendent of Schools, with the concurrence of the Board of Education, and the sanction of the Governor in Council.

42. And be it enacted, That it shall be lawful for any District Council to authorize the establishment of both a female and male School in any School section, each of which shall be subject to the same regulations and obligations as Common Schools generally.

43. And be it enacted, That the Corporate City of Toronto and town of Kingston, shall be considered each a Municipal District for all the purposes of this Act: and the Corporation of each of the said City and Town shall have all the authority and be subject to all the obligations within the limits of each of the said City and Town, respectively, which are conferred and imposed by this Act upon each Council of a District.

44. And be it enacted, That the word "Governor" whenever it occurs in this Act shall include the Governor or any person administering the Government of this Province; and the word "Teacher" shall include Female as well as Male Teachers, except when applied to the Teacher of a Normal or Model School, in which case it shall apply to a Male Teacher only, and that the words "Upper Canada" whenever they occur in this Act shall mean all

that part of this Province, which formerly constituted the Province of Upper Canada.

45.   And be it enacted, That this section and the first ten sections of this Act shall have force and effect immediately after the passing *therefore*, any thing contained in any previous Act to the contrary notwithstanding ; and the remaining sections of this Act, from the eleventh to the forty-fourth inclusive, shall have force and effect upon, from and after the first day of January, one thousand eight hundred and forty-seven, and not before ; and upon, from and after the said day, the Act passed in the seventh year of Her Majesty's Reign, and intituled, *An Act for the establishment and maintenance of Common Schools in Upper Canada*, shall be repealed, excepting in so far as the same repeals any former Act or any part thereof : Provided always, that all penalties incurred under the said Act, shall be collected in the same manner, upon and after the first day of January, one thousand eight hundred and forty-seven, as if the said Act were in force ; Provided also, that all monies which shall remain in the hands of Township, Town or City Superintendents of Schools on the first day of January, one thousand eight hundred and forty-seven, shall immediately thereafter be paid over to the District Superintendents, to be retained and disposed of by them as other moneys remaining in their hands at the end of the year : Provided likewise, that all those divisions of Townships, Towns or Cities which in the said Act are called "School Districts," shall upon and after the said first of January, one thousand eight hundred and forty-seven, be called "School Sections," and be so considered for all the purposes of this Act, until altered in the manner hereby provided.

MILITIA LAW.

—

An Act to repeal certain Laws therein mentioned, to provide for the better defence of this Province, and to regulate the Militia thereof.

(9th June, 1846.)

(1. This section repeals all previous Militia acts.)

2. And be it enacted, That the Militia of this Province shall consist of the male inhabitants thereof, over the age of eighteen years, and under the age of sixty years, being natural born subjects of Her Majesty, or naturalized, and having resided more than six months in this Province ; and the men composing the said Militia shall be divided into two classes, and all such persons between the ages of eighteen and forty years shall belong to and form the first class, and those between the ages of forty and sixty years, shall belong to and form the second class : Provided always, and be it enacted, that in time of peace the Privates of each Regiment of Militia, shall consist of men belonging to the first class only.

3. And be it enacted, That the Governor of this Province may, by Commissions under his hand 'and seal, appoint a sufficient number of Lieutenant-Colonels, Majors, Captains, and other Officers, to train, discipline, and command the Regiments or Battalions of the Militia to be formed under this Act, according to such orders and regulations as shall from time to time be issued by him for that purpose.

4. And be it enacted, That the proportion of the number of Officers to the number of Privates shall not be greater in the said Militia than in Her Majesty's Army; that every Field Officer and Adjutant in the said Militia shall be resident within the limits of his Regimental Division : And that every other Officer shall reside within the limits of his Battalion Division.

5. And be it enacted, That the Officers of Militia so commissioned and appointed, shall rank with Officers of Her Majesty's other Forces serving in this Province as Juniors of their respective ranks.

6. And be it enacted, That the Governor of this Province may, when and in such manner, not inconsistent with this Act, as he shall judge best for carrying the same into effect, divide this Province into Regimental Divisions and Battalion Divisions, and may in like manner from time to time alter the said Regimental or Battalion Divisions and establish others : And notice of such divisions and of all alterations thereof shall be given in such manner as the Governor shall direct : Provided always, that the Cities and Towns Corporate named in the Schedule to this Act, shall be considered as Battalion Divisions as far as regards the Officers to be appointed to Battalions within such Cities or Towns.

7. And be it enacted, That the Lieutenant Colonel of each Battalion of the Militia (including any such Officer commanding a Regiment of only one Battalion) may in like manner divide his Battalion Division into Company Divisions, and may from time to time alter such Company Divisions or any of them, reporting such divisions and alterations forthwith to the Adjutant General, and giving notice thereof and otherwise proceeding with regard to the same, according to the provisions of this Act and such regulations made under it as may be then in force ; and each Company shall be distinguished by a number to be assigned to it.

8. And be it enacted, That each and every person belonging to either class of Militiamen, shall enroll himself with the Captain or other Officer commanding the Company within the limits of which such Militiaman shall then reside, on some one of the first twenty days of the month of June in each and every year, and shall in so enrolling himself state his name, age and residence, and whether he is married or unmarried : And the Captain or other Officer commanding each Company shall cause such enrollment to be made, and shall give at least ten days previous public notice of the day or days (within the period aforesaid) and of the place within the Company Division on and at which he or some other Officer acting under his orders will attend for the purpose of making such enrollment.

9. Provided always, and be it enacted, That in the present year such enrollment shall be made at such time as the Governor shall by any General Order appoint: Provided always, that all Clerks of the Peace, Assessors and persons employed in taking the *Census*, shall at all reasonable times allow the Officers or persons engaged in making such Rolls, free access to all public returns and documents in their custody, and afford them all such other official information as may be required for ascertaining what persons ought to enroll themselves as aforesaid.

10. And be it enacted, That each Officer receiving such enrollment as aforesaid, shall, within eight days after the completion thereof, return the Roll to the Officer Commanding his Battalion, who shall forthwith make a general return of his Battalion to the Adjutant General, and the Adjutant General shall thereupon (in obedience to such order as he shall receive from the Governor,) inform each Officer commanding a Battalion, of the *Quota* or number of men then required for active service; and the Officer commanding each Battalion shall then inform each Officer commanding a Company in such Battalion of the number of men for active service then required.

11. And be it enacted, That on receiving such information as last aforesaid, each Officer commanding a Company shall, by public notice, appoint a place and a day at which he shall require all the Militiamen of the first class to attend for the purpose of determining who among them shall be the men for active service.

12. And be it enacted, That on the day so appointed as last aforesaid such Captain or some Officer under his orders, shall take down the names of all the men of the first class belonging to the Company who shall volunteer for service, and if more than the requisite number shall so volunteer, he shall select such requisite number from those so volunteering, and the men so selected shall be the men for active service: but if less than the requisite number shall volunteer, then the men required to make up such number shall be ballotted for, and the Captain or other Officer aforesaid

shall proceed to ballot for such men in the manner following, or as nearly so as circumstances will allow, that is to say :

He shall write the name of each of the men who have not volunteered, on a slip of paper, and shall fold up the same (all the slips being as nearly as may be of the same size, and folded alike) ; and shall put the said slips into a box and shake them, and shall draw them out one by one, shaking them each time, and reading aloud and marking down each name so drawn, until the number sufficient to form the requisite number shall have been drawn, and he shall then stop : and the men whose names shall have been so drawn shall be those for active service during the term for which the ballot shall be made, leaving to each his lawful claim to exemption if any he shall have ; but in taking the men to form the *Quota*. the unmarried men of the first class shall be first taken, and if they be insufficient, then the unmarried men of the second class, and, if these be insufficient, then the married men of the first class, and lastly the married men of the second class : Provided always, that if part only of the men of any of the descriptions aforesaid be taken, then Volunteers shall be first received and the remainder made up by ballot as aforesaid.

And the Captain or other Officer aforesaid shall make a Return of all his proceedings to the Officer commanding the Battalion, who shall return the same to the Adjutant General, in such form and under such regulations as shall be directed by Militia General Orders : Provided always, that no such selection by volunteering or ballot shall be required, except when the said Militia are called out for active service, according to this Act.

13. And be it enacted, That the said Captain or other Officer aforesaid, shall notify the men who are to serve, of their being so ballotted for active service, and of the period for which they are to serve.

14. And be it enacted, That, in all cases of emergency, it shall be lawful for the Governor to order and direct the men so taken or ballotted for active service to assemble at

D

such place or places as he shall appoint, for the purpose of being formed into Companies and Battalions : and it shall also be lawful for the Governor to designate by name or number the Battalions so to be formed, and to appoint such and so many Officers to train, discipline and command such Companies and Battalions as he may think fit, in conformity with the provisions of this Act as to the proportion between the number of Officers and Privates : Provided always, that the Captains and Subalterns shall be taken from the Regimental Division from which the privates they are appointed to command shall come, as far as the same may be practicable.

15. And be it enacted, That if at any time it shall appear that the number of men for active service, volunteering or ballotted for service in the Militia in any Company Division, does not amount to the number which such division ought to furnish, the deficiency shall be supplied by volunteering or ballot from the men on the Roll of such division, to be ordered and made in the manner hereinbefore provided for ballotting in other cases, or as nearly so as may be practicable.

16. And be it enacted, That the ordinary *Quota* of Militiamen in this Province shall not exceed thirty thousand men, but it shall be lawful for the Governor from time to time to direct such contingent or *Quota* to be increased or diminished, as circumstances may require.

17. Provided always, and be it enacted, That the period for which the Militiamen so called out for actual service shall be respectively liable to serve. shall be regulated as follows, that is to say ; at the end of one year from the time of their being assembled for actual service, one half, to be determined by lot, under the direction of the Officer Commanding the Battalion, shall be permitted to return home, and the other half shall remain for a second year, and then also be permitted to return home ; and the place of those returning home shall from time to time, and as often as occasion shall require, be supplied by a new *Quota* or contingent to be obtained or ballotted for as hereinbefore provided,

so that, excepting the first half, the said Militiamen shall be liable to serve for two years at a time, and not longer : Provided that on every selection of a new *Quota* or contingent, those men who have already served, or who have served most recently, shall not be ballotted for a second term of service until the others of the respective classes have been exhausted.

18. And be it enacted, That in so far as circumstances and the information possessed by the proper authorities will permit, the said Battalion and Company Divisions from which the *Quota* or contingent for active service is to be taken, shall be so made as that no Battalion shall consist of more than ten nor less than four Companies, and no Company of less than sixty nor of more than one hundred and twenty men, exclusive of Non commissioned Officers and Drummers.

19. And be it enacted, That in addition to the *Quotas* or contingents actually organized, the Governor may call out and embody the whole or such part as may appear to him expedient of the Militia of any Regiment, Battalion or Company in this Province, in time of actual War with a Foreign Power, to repel invasion, or other pressing exigency, or for any purpose connected with the preservation of the public peace or the safety of the Province, in such manner as shall to him seem best, and may march the Militia into any part of the Province, and shall also have power to march the Militia or any portion thereof, to any place without the limits of the Province but conterminous therewith, for the attack of any enemy that may have invaded, or may be marching or collected for the purpose of invading this Province, or for the destruction of any vessel or vessels, built or building, or of any Fort, Depot or Magazine, formed or forming, by any Foreign Power at War with the Queen, Her Heirs or Successors, from whence the invasion of this Province may be apprehended, and in no other case or cases whatever.

20. And be it enacted, That whenever a part only of the Militia shall be so called out, it shall and may be lawful

for any person being a private Militiaman to provide and send an approved substitute eligible to serve in the Militia to serve in his stead ; and such substitute being accepted and enrolled for service, shall be liable to all the obligations of the man for whom he is substituted.

21.   And be it enacted, That when the Militia are so called out and embodied, any Officer, Non-Commissioned Officer or Militiaman, belonging to any portion thereof so called out and embodied, who shall begin, excite, cause or join in any mutiny or sedition in the Regiment, Detachment, Troop or Company to which he belongs, or in any other Regiment, Detachment, Troop or Company, whether of Embodied Militia, or of Her Majesty's Regular or Provincial Forces, in any Camp or Post, or upon any party, detachment or guard, on any pretence whatever, shall suffer such punishment other than death or corporal punishment as by a General Court Martial shall be awarded.

22.   And be it enacted, That any Officer, Non-Commissioned Officer or Militiaman, who, being present at any mutiny or sedition, shall not use his utmost endeavours to suppress the same, or coming to the knowledge of such mutiny or sedition, shall not without delay give information thereof to his Commanding Officer, shall suffer such punishment, other than death or corporal punishment, as by a General Court Martial shall be awarded.

23.   And be it enacted, That any Officer, Non-Commissioned Officer or Militiaman, who shall be convicted of having deserted to the enemy, shall suffer death or such other punishment as shall be awarded by a General Court Martial.

24.   And be it enacted, That any Officer, Non-Commissioned Officer or Militiaman, who shall quit or otherwise absent himself from his Regiment, Detachment, Troop or Company, without a furlough from his Commanding Officer, or who shall withdraw himself from the Regiment, Detachment, Troop or Company, into which he has been embodied, in order to attach himself to any other Regiment, Detachment, Troop or Company then in service, whether of the

Militia or of Her Majesty's Regular or Provincial Troops, shall, on being convicted thereof, be punished, (excepting by death or corporal punishment,) according to the nature of his offence, at the discretion of a General Court Martial ; and in case any Officer of the Militia shall knowingly entertain such Non-Commissioned Officer or Militiaman, or shall not, after his being discovered to be a deserter, immediately confine him and give notice to the Regiment, Detachment, Troop or Company in which he last served, he, tho said Officer so offending, shall, on conviction thereof before a General Court Martial, be cashiered : And be it enacted, that if any Officer, Non-Commissioned Officer or Militiaman, shall be convicted of having advised or persuaded any other Officer, Non-Commissioned Officer or Militiaman to desert Her Majesty's Service, he shall suffer such punishment as shall be awarded by a General Court Martial

25. And be it enacted, That the Governor shall have the power to form such men, belonging to the Militia, as shall volunteer for that purpose, into Regiments or other Corps of Militia, Dragoons, Artillery, Rifles or Light Infantry, separate and distinct from other Militia Corps, and to be taken from the different Battalion or Company Divisions aforesaid, in any Regimental Division, and from such local portions thereof as the Governor shall appoint with regard to each such Volunteer Corps, and to appoint the necessary Officers ; and such Corps so constituted, shall be subject to such orders, rules and regulations, with respect to drill, inspection, or other duties, as from time to time may be issued for their efficient organization for actual service, apart from other Militia Corps in the Province, but shall otherwise be liable to the same duties and obligations as other Militia Corps, and subject to the provisions of this Act in like manner : Provided always, that nothing herein contained shall prevent any approved man from serving in any such Volunteer Corps although he be not then ballotted for service in the Militia, provided he shall take upon himself the same obligations and for the same period as if he were then so ballotted for service ; and the obligations so taken upon himself

shall then be as valid and binding and may be enforced against him in the same manner as if he had been ballotted for service as aforesaid.

26. And be it enacted, That the Governor may, by Volunteers as aforesaid, and under like provisions. form a Provincial Naval Corps, and may appoint a Commodore, who shall rank with Lieutenant-Colonels of Militia, and also Captains and Lieutenants of a Provincial Navy, who shall rank with Majors and Captains of the Militia, as Seniors of their respective ranks ; and the Officers and men of such Corps shall be drilled to the exercise of heavy guns, and to the management of gun-boats, in addition to their duties in the use of small arms as a Militia force.

27. And be it enacted, That in case Her Majesty shall be pleased to appoint Inspecting Field Officers of Militia, holding the rank of Field Officer in Her Majesty's other Forces. for any portion or portions of this Province, such Inspecting Field Officers shall respectively have the rank of Colonel of Militia, and shall command the Militia within the Inspection Districts to which they shall be so appointed ; but this grant of the Militia rank of Colonel shall not confer upon these Officers any privilege of rank or authority over any part of Her Majesty's Forces, beyond that which their rank in the Regular Service entitles them to : Provided, that all Colonels serving by Commissions signed by Her Majesty's General Commanding in Chief in British North America, shall, when employed on any duty in conjunction with Colonels serving by commissions from the Governor of this Province, have precedence of such Colonels although the Commissions of the latter be of elder date.

28. And be it enacted, That the First Class of Militia shall be assembled for muster and discipline, for one day in each year, as shall be directed in each division respectively, and such day shall be the twenty-ninth day of June, unless that day be Sunday, in which case the next following day shall be the day for so assembling : Provided always, that the Governor may, by any General Order, dispense with or forbid such assembling in any year and with regard to any division of Militia.

29. And be it enacted, That in case of any sudden emergency, wherein the aid of the said Militia Forces shall be required for the purposes of repelling any invasion, or any other pressing danger or emergency, when there shall be no opportunity of communication with the Governor, it shall be lawful for the Senior Lieutenant Colonel, or other Officer commanding any Regiment of Militia, to call out and assemble the whole, or any portion of the Militia of the Regimental Division in which such Lieutenant Colonel or other Officer shall command, as the case may be, for actual service, and to keep the said Militia, so called out, assembled for actual service until the pleasure of the Governor shall be known.

30. And be it enacted, That the following persons shall be and are hereby excused from actual service in the said Militia, in any case, namely :

The Judges of Her Majesty's Courts of Queen's Bench, or of King's Bench :

The Vice Chancellor :

The Judge of the Court of Vice-Admiralty :

The Judges of the Circuit and District Courts, and Commissioners of Bankrupts :

The Clergy and Ministers of all denominations of Christians :

The Professors in any College or University, and the class of persons known as *Les Freres de la Doctrine Chretienne :*

The Keepers and Guards of the Provincial Penitentiary.

And that the following persons shall be exempted from actual service in the said Militia, except in time of War, Invasion, or Insurrection, but not from enrollment :

The Members of the Executive and Legislative Councils :

The Members of the Legislative Assembly :

The Officers of the said Councils and Assembly, respectively :

The Attorneys and Solicitors General :

The Provincial Secretary, and Assistant Secretaries :

All Civil Officers who shall have been appointed to any. Civil Office in this Province under the Great Seal :

All persons lawfully authorized to practice Physic or Surgery :

All Advocates, Barristers, Solicitors or Attorneys :

Notaries in Lower Canada :

Half-pay and retired Officers of Her Majesty's Army and Navy :

Post Masters and Mail Carriers :

Sea-faring men actually employed in the line of their calling :

Masters of the Public or Common Schools :

Ferry-men :

One Miller for each run of stones in every Grist Mill :

Keepers of Public Toll Gates :

Lock Masters, and Labourers employed in attending to Locks or Bridges on Public Canals :

Members of Fire Companies and of Hook and Ladder Companies :

Constables and Officers of the Courts of Justice, not being such solely by virtue of their office as Non-commissioned Officers of Militia :

Students attending Seminaries, Colleges, Schools, and Academies, who have been attending such at least six months previous to the time at which they might be called upon to do Militia duty :

All persons disabled by bodily infirmity.

Provided always, that such exemption shall not prevent, or be construed to prevent any or every of the above-mentioned persons from holding Commissions as Officers of Militia, or from serving in the said Militia if they shall desire so to do; And provided also, that the Governor may exempt any of the above mentioned persons, or any other persons, from actual service at any time in the said Militia ; Provided further, that no person shall, in any prosecution under this Act, be entitled to claim such exemption unless he shall before the commencement of such prosecution have served.

upon the Captain of the Company in which he ought other·
wise to serve, a notice of his claim to such exemption, and
his affidavit sworn before some Justice of the Peace, of the
facts on which such claim shall be founded ; and in every
case where exemption shall be claimed, as well on the ground
of age as otherwise, the burden of proof shall lie upon the
person making such claim.

31.   And be it enacted, That the persons called Quakers,
Mennonists or Tunkers, who, from scruples of conscience,
decline bearing arms, shall, on certain conditions, be exempt from actual service in the Militia, that is to say :
every person who would otherwise be liable to serve in the
Militia aforesaid, and who shall profess to be one of the
people called Quakers, Mennonists or Tunkers, and shall
produce to the Captain of the Company in which he ought
otherwise to serve, a certificate of his being a Quaker, Mennonist or Tunker, signed by the Clerk, Pastor, Minister or
Elder of such Society, or by three or more of the said people called Quakers, Mennonists or Tunkers, shall be exempt
from actual service in the said Militia for one year, on payment to the said Captain of the sum of five shillings, currency, in time of Peace, and in case of War, Invasion, or
other emergency, when the Militia aforesaid shall be under
orders for actual service, of a sum not exceeding twenty
pounds, currency ; and that in case any such person shall
neglect or refuse so to obtain such exemption, he shall be
liable to the provisions of this Act, and to the same pains
and penalties for any contravention thereof, as if he were
not such Quaker, Mennonist or Tunker ; But nothing herein contained shall be construed to exempt any such person
as aforesaid, from the obligation to enroll himself in his
Company Division as hereinbefore provided, or from the
penalty for not so enrolling himself.

32.   And be it enacted, That within one month after receiving any fine or pecuniary penalty under this Act. the Officer receiving the same shall pay over to the Receiver General of this Province, for the public uses thereof, the monies
he shall have so received ; and if he shall wilfully neglect

or refuse so to do, he shall be liable, upon trial and conviction for such offence, by General Court Martial, to be cashiered; and upon such trial the burden of proof of having
paid over such sum shall be upon the person charged before
such Court Martial.

33.   And be it enacted, That no person who shall have
been an Officer or Non-commissioned Officer in Her Majesty's Regular service, or in the Militia in any part of this
Province, or an Officer in the Militia in any part of Her
Majesty's Dominions, shall be obliged to serve in any in-
ferior station in the Militia of this Province, unless he shall
have been reduced by sentence of a Court Martial, or other
lawful authority, or unless, having been offered the rank
he may have theretofore held as aforesaid, he shall have
refused or neglected to accept the same; and that every
Officer and Non commissioned Officer of Militia shall be
exempt from the obligation of serving as Constable during
the time he shall be such Officer or Non-commissioned
Officer.

34.   And be it enacted, That it shall be lawful for the
Governor to appoint by Commissions under his hand and
seal, one Adjutant General of Militia, and two Deputy Adjutants General, who shall respectively be stationed in such
place and places as the Governor from time to time shall
order and direct, and who shall attend to the issuing of Militia General Orders, the preparation and issuing of Commissions of Militia Officers, to the organization, training,
discipline and management of the said Militia, and perform
the other duties appertaining to the office of Adjutant General of Militia, in obedience to such orders and regulations
as shall be from time to time issued and made by the Govern-
or of this Province.

35.   And be it enacted, That the Adjutant General of
Militia shall have the rank of Colonel of Militia, and the
Deputy Adjutants General shall have the rank of Lieuten-
ant-Colonels of Militia.

36.   And be it enacted, That the Governor may appoint
persons belonging to his Personal Staff, to such Militia

rank as he may think proper to confer, not exceeding the rank of Lieutenant Colonel, independent of, and apart from any rank that may be held by such person in any Regiment or Battalion of Militia in this Province.

37. And be it enacted, That the Governor may from time to time prescribe the uniforms to be worn by the Militia of the Province when on duty upon actual service, and may require Officers of Militia to provide themselves with such books for instruction in their duty as he shall see fit.

38. And be it enacted, That any Officer of Militia who shall not, when called out for actual service in time of war, provide himself with such uniform, including a sword, or who shall when on such actual service appear at any Muster or Inspection of the Battalion or Corps to which he shall belong, without being dressed in such uniform and sword, or who shall not have provided himself with such Books of instruction as may be hereafter required by any Militia General Order, shall be and he is hereby declared to be superseded.

39. And be it enacted, That any Officer of Militia who, in time of peace, shall be guilty of wilful neglect or disobedience of orders, or any act of insubordination, in the performance of his duty, shall on conviction, be liable to pay a fine not less than two pounds, ten shillings, nor more than twenty pounds, besides costs of conviction, or to be dismissed the service, at the discretion of the Court before whom he shall be tried.

40. And be it enacted, That any Militiaman who, in time of peace, shall be guilty of wilful neglect or disobedience of orders at any time, or of any act of insubordination or misconduct, while on parade or engaged in the performance of Militia duty, shall, on conviction, incur a fine of not less than five shillings nor more than ten shillings over and above the costs of conviction ; and in default of payment, and if sufficient distress be to found, shall be liable to imprisonment in the Common Gaol of the District for a term not less than six days, nor more than one month, unless the fine be sooner paid.

41. And be it enacted, That any Officer or Militiaman, who, in time of War, or when the Regiment, Detachment, or Corps to which he shall belong, shall be ordered out for actual service, or any such danger or pressing emergency as aforesaid, shall wilfully refuse or neglect to obey any order, or shall abscond from, or neglect to repair to the place he is ordered to, shall, unless he shall satisfy the Lieutenant Colonel or Officer commanding the Battalion or Corps to which he belongs, that such refusal or neglect arose from sickness, or that he was absent upon leave, as soon as possible be brought to trial before a Court Martial, as hereinafter provided, and shall be liable to be punished by fine, imprisonment or otherwise in the discretion of the Court Martial by whom he shall be tried ; Provided that no such Militiaman shall be flogged in any case whatever.

42. And be it enacted, That every person whether he be or be not in the Militia, and although he be also liable to be tried for the offence by Court Martial, who, at any time whatever, shall sell, barter or pledge, or tender in sale, barter or pledge, or unlawfully make away with any part of the arms or equipments of the said Militia force, or any ammunition or stores, and every person who shall buy or by barter or pledge obtain, or who shall otherwise unlawfully receive, take or detain any portion of the said arms or equipments, or ammunition or stores, shall be deemed guilty of a misdemeanor upon conviction for such offence before any Court of competent jurisdiction, and be liable to be punished accordingly.

43. And be it enacted, That all Officers charged with any offence or offences against the provisions of this Act in time of peace, shall be tried by General Court Martial ; and that the Governor of this Province shall have authority by any Militia General Orders, to assemble such General Court Martial,—the same to consist of one Field Officer of Militia as President, and at least six other Commissioned Officers ; provided that when a Field Officer cannot conveniently be had for such service, a Captain may act as President.

44. Provided always, and be it enacted, That no Officer under the rank of Captain shall sit upon the trial of any Field Officer ; and that the Senior Officer on any Court Martial shall be the President thereof.

45. And be it enacted, That the Governor may appoint a Judge Advocate for every General Court Martial, who shall be entitled to receive for each day upon which the Court Martial shall sit the sum of twenty-five shillings.

46. And be it enacted, That every Militiaman, charged with any offence or offences against the provisions of this Act in time of peace, shall be tried by Regimental Court Martial.

47. And be it enacted, That the Officer commanding the Battalion or Corps to which the offender shall belong, shall have full power and authority, in time of peace, to assemble an Ordinary Court Martial, to be composed of not less than three Officers of the Battalion or Corps, one of whom shall be of the rank of Captain, and upon which Court the Officer who shall assemble the same shall not sit ; and such Court shall have authority to hear and determine all charges that may be brought against any Militiaman for any offence or neglect of duty, contrary to the provisions of this Act.

48. And be it enacted, That the Officer who shall assemble any such Ordinary Court Martial, in time of peace, shall order the Captain or other Officer in Command of the Company to which the Militiaman charged with any offence against the provisions of this Act shall belong, to cause notice in writing to be given to the person so charged, requiring him to appear and answer to any such charge, which notice shall be signed by the Captain or Officer commanding such Company, and may be in the words, or to the effect following :

" You, A. B., are required to attend before an Ordinary " Court Martial of the   of Militia, " which will assemble at
" on the   day of   at
"o'clo k in the forenoon, to answer to a charge which will

"be then and there preferred against you, for (*setting forth*
"*the offence briefly, as the case may be.*")
   "Dated this   day of
   "18   .   (*Signed*,) C. D. Cap-
"tain of (*or* Officer commanding) the
"Company of the   of Militia."
   49. And be it enacted, That no such Militiaman shall
be condemned or liable to answer any charge preferred
against him, unless it be proved at the time appointed for the
trial of the charge, that he was served with a notice as here-
in-before provided, at least four days before the meeting of
the Court ; and that if any such Militiaman, on whom such
notice shall have been served, shall not appear to answer to
the charge preferred against him; the Court may proceed to
the trial of the said charge, and pronounce judgment as if
the person so charged were present and answering to such
charge.
   50. And be it enacted, That the person who shall serve
notices as required by this Act, shall be entitled to receive
four pence for each mile he shall necessarily travel, to effect such service, and one shilling and three pence for such
service, and every person who shall arrest and convey to
prison any Militiaman, in pursuance of the sentence of any
such Court Martial, shall receive the sum of one shilling
and three pence for such arrest, and four pence for each
mile he shall necessarily travel to make the same.
   51. And be it enacted, That the persons who shall be
employed in the summoning witnesses, and in serving notices, and others who shall be entitled under this Act to remu-
neration for any service relating to such Court Martial, shall
be entitled to receive the same from the President of such
Court Martial, to whom it shall be paid by the Adjutant
General, out of such monies as shall be from time to time
advanced to him (by warrant of the Governor addressed to
the Receiver General) for the purpose of defraying the contingent expenses lawfully incurred under this Act; and such
Adjutant General is hereby authorized and required to pay
the same, upon receiving a Pay List signed by the Presi-

dent of such Court Martial, and shall charge the said amount in account with the Government of this Province.

52. And be it enacted, That no Officer serving in the Militia shall sit on any Court Martial upon the trial of any Officer or Soldier serving in any of Her Majesty's other Forces ; nor shall any Officer serving in any of Her Majesty's other Forces sit in Court Martial upon the trial of any Officer or Soldier serving in the Militia.

53. And be it enacted, That no sentence of any General Court Martial shall be carried into effect until the same shall be approved by the Governor of this Province ; and no sentence of any Ordinary Court Martial shall be carried into effect until the same shall be approved by the Officer who shall have assembled such Ordinary Court Martial.

54. And be it enacted, That every such Militia Court Martial (General as well as Ordinary) shall have power to summon witnesses, and to examine such witnesses upon oath, relative to any charge which such Court Martial shall be assembled to try ; and if any witness so summoned shall neglect or refuse to give his attendance or being in attendance shall refuse to give evidence, he may, by such Court Martial, be committed to the Common Gaol of the District in which such Court Martial shall be held, for any term not exceeding eight days.

55. And be it enacted, That in all trials by Militia General Courts Martial, the Judge Advocate, or person officiating as such, shall administer to each Member the oath hereinafter inserted ; and in trials by all other Militia Courts Martial, the same oath shall be administered by the President to the other Members, and afterwards, by any sworn Member, to the President :

" You shall well and truly try, and determine according " to the evidence, the matter now before you, and you shall " duly administer justice therein, according to law, without " partiality, favour or affection : you shall not divulge the " sentence of the Court until it shall be approved by the " Governor, (*or in case of an Ordinary Court Martial, by* "the Officer to whom such approval shall lawfully belong,)

" neither shall you at any time or on any account whatsoever
" disclose or discover the vote or opinion of any particular
" member of the Court Martial, unless required to give evi-
" dence thereof in due course of Law ; So help you God."

And as soon as the said oath shall have been administered
to the respective members, the President of the Court shall
administer to the Judge Advocate, or person officiating as
such at a General Court Martial, an oath in the following
words :

"I, A. B., do swear, that I will not, on any account what-
" soever, discover the vote or opinion of any particular
" Member of this Court Martial, unless required to give evi-
" dence thereof as a witness, by a Court of Justice or a Court
" Martial, in due course of Law. So help me God."

56. And be it enacted, That all persons who shall give evidence before any Court Martial, shall be examined on oath
in the following words :

" The evidence which you shall give before the Court,
" shall be the truth, the whole truth, and nothing but the
" truth. So help you God."

57. And be it enacted, That any person who shall use
menacing words, signs or gestures in the presence of any
Court Martial, or shall cause any disorder or riot so as to
disturb its proceedings, shall be liable to be imprisoned,
upon the warrant of the President of the Court, in the
Common Gaol of the District in which such Court shall sit,
for any period not exceeding eight days, at the discretion of
such Court Martial.

58. And be it enacted, That the Governor may, if he
shall think proper, when any complaint shall be made
against any Officer of the Militia, or when any application
shall be made to him in that behalf, assemble a Militia General Court Martial, or may, at any other time, appoint a
Court of Inquiry, to consist of at least three Militia Officers,
to examine into and report upon such complaint, or upon
the grounds of any such application, or cause of inquiry.

59. And be it enacted, That all persons imprisoned

under sentence or order of any Court Martial in time of peace, shall, by the Warrant of the President of such Court Martial, under his hand and seal, specifying the cause of the committal of such persons, be committed to the Common Gaol of the District in which the Court Martial shall be held, and upon such Warrant shall be received and kept by the gaoler for the period therein mentioned.

60. And be it enacted, That if any person shall wilfully interrupt or molest any portion of the said Militia Force whilst on any lawful duty, it shall be lawful for the Officer present and in command thereof, to cause such person to be arrested and taken under guard of any one or more Militiamen, before any one of Her Majesty's Justices of the Peace, who, after complaint made upon oath, shall, upon summary conviction, sentence such offender to pay a fine not exceeding ten shillings, or in default of payment and of sufficient distress. may commit the offender for a period not exceeding eight days, to the Common Gaol of the District, if the fine be not sooner paid.

61. And be it enacted, That when Her Majesty's Regular Forces, or the Militia aforesaid, shall be on a march within this Province, and billetted as hereinafter mentioned, each and every householder therein shall, when required, furnish them with house-room, fire and utensils for cooking, and candles; and in cases of emergency, by actual invasion or otherwise, it shall and may be lawful for the Officer commanding the Regiment, Battalion or Detachment of Troops or Militia, to direct and empower any Officer or Non-Commissioned Officer of the same, or other person, having first obtained a Warrant for such purpose from a Justice of the Peace, to impress and take such horses, carriages, or oxen as the service may require, the use of which shall be thereafter paid for at the usual rate of hire for such horses, carriages or oxen.

62. And be it enacted, That when the said Troops of Her Majesty, or Militia, or any Regiment, Battalion, or Detachment of the same, are on a march as aforesaid, the Officer or Non-commissioned Officer commanding such

E

Troops or Militia, or such Regiment, Battalion or Detachment thereof, shall present to a Justice of the Peace a requisition in writing to such Justice to billet, who shall immediately thereupon so billet the said Troops or Militia as to facilitate their march, and in such manner as may be most commodious to the inhabitants ; and that every inhabitant householder who shall refuse to receive the said Troops or Militia, so billeted upon them as aforesaid, or to furnish them with lodging and articles mentioned in the next preceding section, shall, for every such offence, forfeit and pay a sum not exceeding forty shillings ; And no Officer shall be obliged to pay for his lodging where he shall be regularly billeted ; but each householder upon whom such soldiers are billeted, shall receive from Government for each Non commissioned Officer, Drummer and Private of Infantry, a daily rate of four pence, and for each Cavalry soldier, whose horse shall be also provided with stabling and forage, a daily rate of ten pence ; and every Officer or Non-commissioned Officer to whom it belongs to receive, or who does actually receive the pay for any Officers or Soldiers shall, every four days, or before they shall quit their quarters, if they shall not remain so long as four days, settle the just demands of all householders, victuallers, or other persons upon whom such Officers and Soldiers are billeted, out of their pay and subsistence money, before any part of the said pay or subsistence money be distributed to them respectively, provided such demands do not exceed in amount their pay and subsistence money for the time, credit beyond which is not to be granted.

63. And be it enacted, That when the safety of this Province shall require that the said Troops of Her Majesty, or Militia, or any Regiment, Corps or Detachment of the same should be cantoned in any part or parts of this Province, then and in such case it shall and may be lawful for any Justice of the Peace in the respective Districts where such Troops or Militia may be cantoned, upon receiving an order from the Commander of the said Troops or Militia, or on a requisition from the Officer commanding

any such cantonment, to quarter and billet, and the said
Justice is hereby required to quarter and billet the Officers,
Non-commissioned Officers Drummers and Privates of the
said Troops or Militia, upon the several inhabitant householders, as near as may be to the place of cantonment,
avoiding as much as possible to incommode the said inhabitants, and taking due care to accommodate the said Troops
or Militia ; and if any inhabitant householder shall refuse
to receive such Troops or Militia, so billeted on him as
aforesaid, and to furnish them with the lodging and articles
hereinbefore mentioned, he shall for each and every offence
forfeit and pay a sum not exceeding forty shillings ; and if
any inhabitant shall consider himself aggrieved by having a
greater number of the said Troops or Militia billeted upon him
than he ought to bear in proportion to his neighbours, by
the said Justice, then on complaint being made to two or
more Justices of the District where such Troops or Militia
shall be cantoned, it shall and may be lawful for such Justices, and they are hereby authorized to relieve such inhabitant, by ordering such and so many of the said Troops or
Militia to be removed and quartered upon such other person
or persons as they shall see cause, and such other person or
persons shall be obliged, under a penalty not exceeding
forty shillings, to receive such Troops or Militia accordingly : Provided that no Justice or Justices of the Peace,
having any Military Office or Commission in the said
Troops or Militia, shall directly or indirectly be concerned
in the quartering or billeting of any Officer, Non-commissioned Officer, Soldier or Soldiers of the Regiment, Corps or
Detachment under the immediate command of such Justice
or Justices : Provided always, that nothing in this Act contained shall be construed to authorize the quartering or billeting of any Troops or Militia, either on a march or in
cantonment, in any Convent or Nunnery of any Religious
Order of Females, or to oblige any such Religious Order to
receive such Troops or Militia, or to furnish them with
lodging or house-room.

61. And be it enacted, That when the said Troops of

Her Majesty, or Militia, or any part of them, shall be so cantoned as aforesaid, any Justice of the Peace of and in the District where such cantonment is made, upon receiving an order from the Commander of the said Troops or Militia in that behalf, or a Requisition in writing from the Officer commanding that cantonment, for such and so many carriages as may be requisite and necessary for the said Troops or Militia, shall and may, and he is hereby required to issue his Warrant to such person or persons as may be possessed of carriages, horses or oxen within his jurisdiction, requiring him or them to furnish the same for the service aforesaid; and if any such person or persons shall neglect or refuse, after receiving such Warrant, to furnish his or their carriage or carriages, horses or oxen for that service, each and every such person or persons shall forfeit and pay a sum not exceeding forty shillings : and the said carriages, horses or oxen may be impressed and taken for such service; Provided always, that such carriage or carriages, horses or oxen, or the carriage or carriages, horses or oxen mentioned in the previous clauses or sections of this Act, shall not be compelled to proceed more than thirty miles, unless in cases where other carriages, horses or oxen cannot immediately be had to replace them; and such carriages, horses or oxen shall be paid for at the usual rate of hire.

65. And be it enacted, That in cases of emergency, when it may be necessary to provide proper and speedy means for the conveyance by water of the said Troops of Her Majesty, or Militia, and also for their ammunition, stores, provisions and baggage, any Justice of the Peace of and in the District where such Troops or Militia may be either on a march or in cantonment, upon receiving a Requisition in writing from the Officer commanding such Troops or Militia, for such boats or other craft as may be requisite for the conveyance of the said Troops or Militia, and their ammunition, stores, provisions and baggage, shall and may and he is hereby required to issue his Warrant to such person or persons as may be possessed of such boats or

other craft, within his jurisdiction, requiring him or them to furnish the same for that service, at and after the rate of payment to be allowed by the said Justice, not exceeding the usual rate of hire for such boats or other craft ; and if any such person or persons shall neglect or refuse, after receiving such Warrant, to furnish his or their boats or craft for that service, such and every such person or persons shall forfeit and pay a sum not exceeding five pounds, and such boats or other craft may be impressed and taken for such service.

66. Provided always, and be it enacted, That if any Officer of Militia shall be guilty of partiality in having exempted any person or persons from such service as aforesaid, without being legally authorized so to do, or in having commanded others to perform such service out of their turn of duty, or shall in any way misuse the power in the five next preceding sections vested in him, he shall for such offence incur a penalty not exceeding five pounds, to be recovered before any two Justices of the Peace, or may be tried by Court Martial and punished in the discretion of the Court.

67. And be it enacted, That no person who shall have been dismissed from Her Majesty's Army or from the Militia, by sentence of a General Court Martial, shall be allowed to hold a Commission in the Militia of this Province.

68. And be it enacted, That the penalties imposed by this Act, and for the recovery of which special provision is not hereinbefore made, may be recovered and enforced before any two or more Justices of the Peace nearest to the place wherein the offence shall have been committed or the offender shall be found, and on the oath of any credible witness or witnesses, or of the informer or prosecutor, to whom no part of the penalty shall in any case belong : and all such penalties, when not otherwise provided for, may be received by such Justices or one of them, and shall be accounted for and paid over for public uses, in the same manner as other penalties received by Justices of the Peace.

69. And be it enacted, That all pecuniary penalties and forfeitures by this Act inflicted, or authorized to be imposed, shall be levied and recovered by distress and sale of the offender's goods and chattels, by warrant under the hand and seal of the Justice of the Peace or of one of the Justices of the Peace, or under the Warrant of the Court, before whom the offender shall have been convicted; and such Justice or Court is hereby empowered and required to issue such Warrant, and in default of sufficient distress, to commit the offender to Gaol by a like Warrant for the period hereinbefore provided in the case; and every Sheriff, Gaoler or other Officer to whom any such Warrant shall be addressed shall obey the same according to the tenor thereof; and the overplus, if any, of the money arising by any such distress and sale shall be returned, upon demand, to the owner or owners of such goods and chattels, deducting therefrom the costs and charges of such distress and sale; and the said penalties and forfeitures shall be paid into the hands of the Receiver-General, for the public uses of this Province.

70. And be it enacted and declared, That the Governor of this Province may issue Her Majesty's pardon for any offence or offences against the provisions of this Act, and may remit any fines or other penalties incurred for any such offence or offences.

71. And be it enacted, That if the statement in any oath or affirmation taken or made in pursuance of this Act, shall, to the knowledge of the person making the same, be false, such person shall be guilty of wilful and corrupt perjury; and whenever an oath is required by this Act, a solemn affirmation may be made instead thereof, if the party of whom the oath would be required be one of those entitled by law to make affirmation.

72. And be it enacted, That no complaint or prosecution shall be brought against any person or persons for any fine or penalty hereinbefore imposed, unless the same be commenced within six months next after the offence committed, except in cases of desertion, or harbouring, concealing, aiding or abetting Deserters, or buying, taking in ex-

change or concealing arms or accoutrements delivered to Militia.

73. And be it enacted, That if any action shall be brought against any person or persons for anything done in pursuance of this Act, the same shall be commenced within six months next after the fact committed. and not afterwards : And the Defendant or Defendants in every such action or suit may plead the general issue and give this Act and the special matter in evidence : And if judgment shall be given for the Defendant or Defendants in any such action or suit, or if the Plaintiff or Plaintiffs shall be nonsuited or discontinue his or their action or suit, after the Defendant or Defendants shall have appeared, the Defendant or Defendants shall have treble costs and have the like remedy for the same as any Defendant hath in other cases to recover costs by law.

74 And be it enacted, That all Commissions to Officers of Militia shall be transmitted by the Adjutant General, or one of the Deputy Adjutants General of Militia, to the Lieutenant Colonel or Officer commanding any Corps, to be delivered to the respective Officers appointed to such Corps.

75. And be it enacted, That it shall be the duty of the Adjutant General to cause to be prepared and printed and transmitted to the several Officers of Militia, who may, under the provisions of the Act, have occasion for the same, proper Blank Forms for all Returns and other proceedings required under this Act.

76. And be it enacted, That when, and so often as the words " Governor," or " Governor of this Province," are used in this Act, the same shall be held to mean and signify the Governor, Lieutenant Governor or person administering the Government of this Province, or any Deputy by him lawfully appointed to perform the function to which the enactment may relate ; and the words " Lower Canada," shall mean all that part of this Province formerly constituting the Province of Lower Canada, and the words " Upper Canada" shall mean all that part of this Province formerly constitut-

ing the Province of Upper Canada ; and the words " Militiaman," or " Militiamen," shall include Non-commissioned Officers, Drummers and Privates of the Militia ; and any duty hereby assigned to any Officer, may, if there be then no such Officer, be performed by the Officer next in rank on whom his command or duties shall have for the time devolved, unless in either case there be some thing in the subject or context inconsistent with such construction ; and whenever power is given to any Officer or person to do any act, or perform any duty, all such powers shall be understood to be given as shall be requisite for the proper doing or performance thereof ; and generally all words, phrases and provisions herein contained shall receive such fair and liberal construction as shall be best calculated to give full effect to this Act, according to its true intent, spirit and meaning.

77. And be it enacted, That this Act shall remain and be in force for the period of three years, and thence to the end of the next ensuing Session of Parliament, and no longer : Provided always nevertherless, that if at the time this Act would accordingly expire there shall be War between Her Majesty, Her Heirs or Successors and the United States of America, then and in such case this Act shall continue and be in force until the end of the Session of Parliament next ensuing the Proclamation of Peace and no longer.

SCHEDULE.

Cities and Towns Corporate referred to in the sixth Section of this Act.

QUEBEC,	MONTREAL,	TORONTO,
	HAMILTON,	
KINGSTON,	BYTOWN,	LONDON.

PROVINCIAL DUTIES ACT.

—

An Act to alter and amend the Laws imposing Provincial Duties of Customs.

[18th May, 1846.

WHEREAS it is expedient to encourage the transport of Foreign Produce through the Canals of this Province, and to make certain changes in the Duties of Customs now imposed : Be it therefore enacted by the Queen's Most Excellent Majesty, by and with the advice and consent of the Legislative Council and of the Legislative Assembly of the Province of Canada, constituted and assembled by virtue of and under the authority of an Act passed in the Parliament of the United Kingdom of Great Britain and Ireland, and intituled, *An Act to Re-unite the Provinces of Upper and Lower Canada, and for the Government of Canada,* and it is hereby enacted by the authority of the same, That so soon as an Act shall be passed during this year, by the Imperial Parliament, altering the Laws regulating the importation of Wheat, Maize and other grain into the United Kingdom, it shall be lawful for the Governor of this Province by Proclamation to make known the same ; and that the third Section of this Act, and every matter and thing contained therein, and the Schedule hereunto annexed, marked A, shall, and they are hereby enacted and declared to be in force upon, from and after the day of the date of such Proclamation, and not before.

2. And be it enacted, That upon, from and after the day of the date of such Proclamation, the Act of the Parliament of this Province, passed in the sixth year of Her Majesty's Reign, intituled, *An Act to impose a Duty on Foreign Wheat imported into this Province ;* and also so much of an Act passed in the last Session of this Parliament, intituled, *An Act for granting Provincial Duties of Customs,* as relates to the Duties on Maize or Indian Corn, shall be, and the same are hereby repealed, and that in lieu thereof, and of all other Duties of Customs imposed by any Provincial Act on such articles, there shall be raised, levied, collected and paid

unto Her Hajesty, Her Heirs and Successors, upon the articles mentioned in the Schedule A, to this Act annexed, the several Duties of Customs respectively inserted, described and set forth therein.

3. And be it enacted, That Foreign Wheat imported into this Province for exportation, or to be ground for exportation, and Foreign Maize or Indian Corn imported into this Province for exportation, may be imported without payment of any duty under this Act, at such Ports within this Province, and subject to such regulations, either by payment of duties in the first instance, and subsequent return thereof, or by bonds being given, conditioned for the exportation of such Wheat, or the Flour made therefrom, or of any Maize or Indian Corn, as the Governor in Council shall from time to time make and appoint for the purpose of preventing any Wheat, Maize or Indian Corn so imported into this Province, from being used or consumed therein without payment of duty.

4. And be it enacted, That from and after the passing of this Act, instead of all other Duties of Customs imposed by any Provincial Act on such articles, there shall be raised, levied, collected and paid unto Her Majesty, Her Heirs and Successors upon the several articles named in the Schedule B, to this Act annexed, the several Duties of Customs respectively inserted, described and set forth in the said Schedule ; Provided always, that nothing in this Act contained shall extend to repeal any tonnage duty, or any duty except such as is imposed on the articles in the said Schedules A and B set forth.

5. And be it enacted, That the duties by this Act imposed, shall be deemed to be duties within the meaning of the Act passed during the last Session of this Parliament, and intituled, *An Act to provide for the management of the Customs and of matters relating to the Collection of the Provincial Revenue*, subject to the provisions of which Act, and of this Act, the said duties shall be ascertained, raised, levied, collected, paid and recovered under the same provisions of law as duties on like articles now are ascertained, raised,

levied, collected, paid and recovered, and until some other
Act or Acts shall be passed for the general regulation of the
Customs, in which case all the duties hereby imposed shall
be ascertained, raised, levied, collected, paid and recovered
under the provisions of such Act or Acts.

6. And be it enacted, That all sums of money which
shall arise from the duties hereby imposed shall be paid to
the Receiver General by the Collectors and other Officers
and persons by whom the same shall have been received,
and shall form part of the Consolidated Revenue Fund of the
Province, and shall be accounted for to Her Majesty, Her
Heirs and Successors through the Lords Commissioners of
Her Majesty's Treasury for the time being, in such manner
and form as Her Majesty, Her Heirs and Successors shall
be pleased to direct.

7. And be it enacted, That all sums of money which
shall arise from the duties hereby imposed and set forth in
words and figures in the Schedules to this Act shall be
sterling money, and payable in such coins as may be lawfully current in this Province and equivalent to the amount
of sterling money to which such duties may amount in any
case ; and the weights and measures in the said Schedules
mentioned and set forth shall be the Imperial weights and
measures now by law established in the United Kingdom of
Great Britain and Ireland ; and in all cases where the said
duties are imposed according to any specific quantity or any
specific value, the same shall be deemed to apply in the
same proportion to any greater or less quantity or value.

8. And be it enacted, That all Foreign Wheat, or
salted or cured meat, for the use of the Fisheries in the
Gulf of St. Lawrence, shall be free of duty, subject to
such regulations as may from time to time be made by
the Governor of this Province in Council, for the purpose
of ascertaining that such articles are *bona fide* intended to
be applied to the use of such Fisheries.

9. And be it enacted, That so much of the Act passed
in the seventh year of Her Majesty's Reign, and intituled,
An Act to continue for a limited time the duties imposed on

Agricultural Produce and Live Stock imported into this Province, as now remains in force, shall be and is hereby continued and made permanent.

10. And be it enacted, That this Act may be amended or repealed by any Act to be passed in the present session of the Legislature.

SCHEDULE A.

Each Imperial quarter of Foreign Wheat, not intended for exportation, or to be ground into flour and the flour exported, three shillings.

Each quarter (of four hundred and eighty pounds weight) of Maize or Indian Corn, not intended for exportation, three shillings.

SCHEDULE B.

Muscovado and Clayed Sugar, Bastard Sugar, and all other Sugars not refined, per hundred weight, seven shillings and six pence.

Dye woods of all kinds, one *per centum ad valorem.*

Leather, or Leather Manufactures imported by sea, or inland from any British Possession in North America, five *per centum ad valorem.*

UPON THE FOLLOWING ARTICLES IMPORTED OTHERWISE THAN BY SEA, OR INLAND FROM ANY BRITISH POSSESSION IN NORTH AMERICA :

Goat Skins, tanned, tawed or in any other way dressed, per dozen, five shillings.

Lamb or Sheep Skins, tanned, tawed or in any way dressed, per dozen, two shillings and six pence.

Calf Skins, tanned, tawed or in any way dressed, per pound, four pence.

Kip Skins, tanned, tawed or in any way dressed, per pound, two pence.

Harness Leather, Upper Leather, and Sole Leather, per pound, one penny and one half-penny.

Leather cut into Shapes, per pound, four pence.

LEATHER MANUFACTURES.

Womens' Boots, Shoes and Calashes of Leather, per dozen pairs, five shillings.

Womens' Boots and Shoes, of Silk, Satin, Jean, or other
Stuffs, Kid or Morocco, per dozen pairs, five shillings.
Girls' Boots, Shoes and Calashes of Leather, under seven
inches in length, per dozen pairs, two shillings.
Girls Boots and Shoes, of Silk, Satin, Jean or other Stuffs,
Kid or Morocco, per dozen pairs, two shillings.
Mens' Boots, per pair, two shillings.
Mens' Shoes, per pair, six pence.
Boys' Boots, under eight inches in length, per pair, nine
pence.
Boys' Shoes, under eight inches in length, per pair, four
pence.

PRESENT BRITISH TARIFF.
—

The following are the duties on Foreign Grain and Flour
imposed by the Customs Act passed during the last Session
of the Imperial Parliament:—

Maize or Indian Corn, per quarter - - 1s 0d

Maize meal, the cwt. - - - - - - - 0 6

Wheat :—Whenever the average price of wheat made up
and published in the manner required by law, shall
be, for every quarter,

Under 48s. the duty per		50s. and under 51s.	7 0
quarter shall be, -	10 0	51s. and under 52s.	6 0
48s. and under 49s.	9 0	52s. and under 53s.	5 0
49s. and under 50s.	8 0	53s. and under 54s.	4 0

Barley, beer or bigg ;—Whenever the average price of barley, made up and published in the manner required by
law, shall be, for every quarter,

Under 26s. the duty per		28s. and under 29s.	3 6
quarter shall be,	5 0	29s. and under 30s.	3 0
26s. and under 27s.	4 6	30s. and under 31s.	2 6
27s. and under 28s.	4 0	31s. and upwards.	2 0

Oats :—Whenever the average price of oats, made up and
published in the manner required by law, shall be, for
every quarter,

Under 18s. the duty per		20s. and under 21s.	2 6
quarter shall be,	4 0	21s. and under 22s.	2 0
18s. and under 19s.	3 6	22s. and upwards,	1 6
19s. and under 20s.	3 0		

Rye, Pease, and Beans ;—For every quarter,

A duty equal in amount to the duty payable on a quarter of barley.

Wheat meal and flour ;—For every barre', being 196 lbs.

A duty equal in amount to the duty payable on thirty-eight gallons and a half of wheat.

Oatmeal ;—For every quantity of 131½ lbs.

A duty equal in amount to the duty payable on a quarter of oats.

GOVERNMENT OF GREAT BRITAIN.

First Lord of the Treasury—Lord John Russell.

Lord Chancellor—Lord Cottenham.

President of the Council—The Marquis of Lansdowne.

Secretary of State for the Colonies—The Earl Grey.

Secretary of State for Foreign Affairs—Viscount Palmerston.

Secretary of State for the Home Department—Sir George Grey, Bart.

Chancellor of the Exchequer—Right Hon. Charles Wood.

First Lord of the Admiralty—The Earl of Auckland.

President of the Board of Control—Sir John Cam Hobhouse.

President of the Board of Trade—The Earl of Clarendon.

Lord Privy Seal—The Earl of Minto.

Chief Commissioner of Woods and Forests—Lord Morpeth.

Chancellor of the Duchy of Lancaster—Lord Campbell.

Postmaster-General—The Marquis of Clanricarde.

Master-General of the Ordnance—The Marquis of Anglesey.

Secretary of War—Right Hon. Fox Maule.

Paymaster-General of the Forces and Treasurer of the Navy—Right Hon. Thomas Babington Macaulay.

Vice-President of the Board of Trade—Right Hon. Thomas Milner Gibson.

Master of the Mint—Right Hon. Richard Lalor Sheil.

Attorney-General—John Jervis, Esq.

Solicitor-General—David Dundas, Esq.

Judge Advocate-General—Charles Buller, Esq., who, it is understood, also performs the duties of an Under-Secretary of the Colonies.

Surveyor-General of the Ordnance—Colonel Charles Richard Fox.

Clerk of the Ordnance—Lieut. Colonel the Hon. George Anson.

Under Secretary for the Colonies—Benjamin Hawes, Esq.

Under Secretary for Foreign Affairs—Right Hon. Edward John Stanley.

Lord Chamberlain of the Household—The Earl Spencer.

Lord Steward of the Household—The Earl Fortesque.

Master of the Horse—The Duke of Norfolk.

Controller of the Household—Lord Arthur Marcus Cecil Hill.

Vice-Chamberlain of the Household—Lord Edward George Fitzalan Howard.

Clerk Marshal and Chief Equerry—Lord Alfred Paget.

Mistress of the Robes—The Duchess of Sutherland.

Lord Advocate of Scotland—The Right Hon. Andrew Rutherford.

Solicitor-General of Scotland—Thomas Maitland, Esq.

Lord Lieutenant of Ireland—The Earl of Besborough.

Chief Secretary to the Lord Lieutenant of Ireland—Right Hon. Henry Labouchere.

Lord Chancellor of Ireland—Right Hon. Mazierre Brady.

Attorney-General for Ireland—Right Hon. R. Moore.

Solicitor General for Ireland—James H. Monaghan, Esq.

Under Secretary to the Lord Lieutenant—Thomas Nicholas Reddington, Esq.

GOVERNMENT OF CANADA.

His Excellency the Right Hon. the Earl of Elgin and Kincardine, Captain General and Governor-in-Chief of Her Majesty's Provinces of Canada, New Brunswick, Nova Scotia, and of the Island of Prince Edward and Governor General of all Her Majesty's Provinces on the Continent of North America, and of the Island of Prince Edward.

EXECUTIVE COUNCIL.

Hons. Dominick Daly, *Provincial Secretary ;* William H. Draper, *Attorney General,* C. W. ; James Smith, *Attorney General,* C. E ; Wm. Morris, *Receiver General ;* D. B. Papineau, *Commissioner of Crown Lands ;* William Cayley, *Inspector General.*

PUBLIC OFFICERS.

Jonn H. Cameron, Esqr., *Solicitor General,* C. W, ; Joseph Andre Taschereau, Esqr., *Solicitor General,* C. E. ; R. A. Tucker, Esqr., *Registrar ;* William B. Robinson, Esq., *Chief Commissioner of Public Works ;* Thomas A. Begly, Esq., *Secretary do. ;* Colonel Young, *Adjutant General ;* Lt. Col. McDonell, *Deputy Adjutant General,* C. W.; Lt. Col. Tache, *Deputy Adjt. General,* C. E. Christopher Dunkin, Esqr., *Assistant Secretary,* C. E. ; James Hopkirk, Esqr., *Assistant Secretary,* C. W.; Joseph Cary, Esqr., *Deputy Inspector General ;* T. A. Stayner, Esq., *Deputy Postmaster General ;* Rev. E. Ryerson, *Superintendant of Common Schools,* C. W.

COURT OF QUEEN'S BENCH.—Hon. J. B. Robinson, *Chief Justice ;* Hon. J. B. Macaulay, Jonas Jones, Archibald McLean, and C. A. Hagerman, *Puisne Judges.*

COURT OF CHANCERY.—The Governor General *Chancellor ;* Hon. R. S. Jameson, *Vice Chancellor ;* J. G. Spragge, Esq., *Master and Registrar.*

QUEEN'S COUNSEL.—Sir Allan Napier Macnab, Knt , and

Robert Baldwin, Henry John Boulton, Henry Sherwood, James E. Small, John Prince, G. M. Boswell, S. B. Harrison and John H. Cameron, Esqrs.

COURT OF PROBATE.—Robert E. Burns, Esq., *Official Principal;* Charles Fitzgibbon, *Registrar.*

PRACTICE COURT.—William Heward, Esq., *Clerk to Judge in Chambers.*

LEGISLATIVE COUNCIL.

—

Hon. R. E. CARON, *Speaker.*

Hon. R. S. Jameson,	Hon. P. H. Knowlton,
" P. B. DeBlaquiere,	" Thomas McKay,
" Peter McGill,	" Gabriel Roy,
" R. B. Sullivan,	" P. H. Moore,
" William Morris,	" Robert Dickson,
" George Pemberton,	" Amable Dionne,
" Alexander Fraser,	" Joseph Dionne,
" Barthelemi Joliette,	" George J. Goodhue,
" James Crooks,	" L. P. Sherwood,
" Adam Fergusson,	" William Walker,
" John Fraser,	" Christopher Widmer,
" John Macaulay,	" J. Æmilius Irving,
" John Hamilton,	" Louis Massue,
" F. P. Bruneau.	" P. B. de Boucherville,
" John McDonald,	" John Neilson,
" Adam Ferrie,	" James Morris.
" J. B. Tache,	

LEGISLATIVE ASSEMBLY.

—

Beauharnois	E Colville	Carleton	—Lyon
Bellechasse	Dr Laterrière	Chambly	E Lacoste
Berthier	D M Armstrong	Champlain	L Guillet
Bonaventure	J L Boutillier	Cornwall	J H Cameron
Brockville	G Sherwood	Dorchester	J A Taschereau
Bytown	Wm Stewart	Drummond	R N Watts

F

Dundas	G Macdonald	Northumberland N Riding G	
Durham	J T Williams		B Hall
Essex	John Prince	Ottawa	Hon D B Papi-
Frontenac	Henry Smith	neau	
Gaspe	R Christie	Oxford	R Riddell
Glengarry	J S McDouald	Portneuf	L T Drummond
Grenville	Dr Jessup	Prescott	N Stewart
Haldimand	D Thompson	Prince Edw	S Conger
Halton E R	G Chalmers	Quebec City	J Chabot & T
Halton W R	James Webster		C Aylwin
Hamilton	Sir A N Macnab	Do Co	P C Chauveau
Hastings	E Murney	Richelieu	Dr Nelson
Huntingdoh	B H Lemoine	Rimouski	L Bertrand
Huron	Hon W Cayley	Rouville	T Franchere
Kamouraska	A Berthelot	Russell	A Petrie
Kent	Joseph Woods	Saguenay	A N Morin
Kingston	J A Macdonald	Shefford	S Foster
Lanark	M Cameron	Sherbrooke Town	E Hale
Leeds	Ogle R Gowan	Do Co	S Brooks
Leinster	J De Witt	Simcoe	W B Robinson
Len & Ad	B Seymour	Stanstead	J McConnell
Lincoln N R	W H Merritt	Stormont	D Æ McDonald
Lincoln S R	J Cummings	St Hyacinthe	T Boutillier
L'Islet	E P Tache	St Maurice	— Desaulniers
London	Hon W H Draper	Terrebonne	L H Lafontaine
Lotbiniere	Joseph Laurin	Three Rivs	Hon D B Viger
Megantic	Hon D Daly	Toronto	H Sherwood &
Middlesex	E Ermatinger		W H Boulton
Missisquoi	Hon J Smith	Two Mounts	W H Scott
Montmorency	J Cauchon	Vaudreuil	J P Lantier
Montreal City	G Moffatt & S	Vercheres	J Leslie
De Bleury		Wentworth	Dr Smith
Montreal Co	A Jobin	Yamaska	Dr Rousseau
Niagara	W H Dickson	York 1st R	J H Price
Nicolet	P A Methot	York 2nd R	G Duggan
Norfolk	I W Powell	York 3rd R	G Munro
Northumberland S Riding A		York 4th R	Robt Baldwin
H Meyers			

LIST OF POST OFFICES IN CANADA,

WITH THE DISTRICTS IN WHICH THEY ARE SITUATED, AND THE NAMES OF THE POSTMASTERS.

Name of Office.	District.	Postmaster.
Abbotsford	Montreal	E. Fisk
Adelaide	London	J. Hoare,
Adolphustown	Prince Edward	D. McWhirter
Adjala	Simcoe	James Hart
Albion	Home	Samuel Walford
Aldborough	London	John McDougald
Alexandar	Eastern	A. McDonell
Ameliasburg	Prince Edward	O. Roblin
Amherstburgh	Western	James Kevill
Amiens	London	James McKirdy
Ancaster	Gore	James Chep
Arnprior	Bathurst	Alex. Young
Asphodel	Colborne	Thomas Walker
Aylmer	London	Philip Hodgkinson
Aylmer	Montreal	Jno. McDonald
Ayr	Gore	Robert Wyllie
Acton	Do.	Robert Swan
Allanburg	Niagara	John Rannie
Amherst Island	Midland	A. Brown
Addison	Johnstown	Jno. Wood
Alnwick	Newcastle	
Babyville	Montreal	Humphrey Nesbitt
Barnston	Do.	A A Adams
Barrie	Simcoe	John McWatt
Bath	Midland	W J McKay
Batiscan	Three Rivers	J B F Filteau
Bayham	London	Thomas Springall
Beachville	Brock	W Ross McAulay
Beamsville	Niagara	Jno Brown Osborne
Beauharnois	Montreal	H Bogue
Beaverton	Home	—— Cameron
Becancour	Three Rivers	Frs Beauchemin
Bedford	Montreal	Nelson Adams

Name of Office.	District.	Postmaster.
Ballinaford	Wellington	Thomas C Stephens
Berlin	Wellington	William Davidson
Belleville	Victoria	Alex. Menzies
Berthier	Montreal	J F G Couter
Beverley	Johnstown	John Warren
Bloomfield	Prince Edward	Philip Clarke
Bolton	Montreal	J Merry
Bond Head	Simcoe	Henry R Archer
Bradford	Simcoe	Thomas Maconkey
Brantford	Gore	William Walker
Brighton	Newcastle	Jos. Lockwood
Brockville	Johnstown	H Jones
Brock	Home	Thos Hill
Brome	Montreal	N Pettes
Brompton	St. Francis	W S Addison
Brougham	Home	R Taun
Buckingham	Montreal	Jos Wilson
Burford	Brock	Wm M Whitehead
Burritt's Rapids	Johnstown	S Burritt
Bytown	Bathurst	G W Baker
Beloeil	Montreal	Louis Tache
Bristol	Do.	W King
Cacona	Quebec	J B Beaubien
Caledon	Home	George Bell
Caledonia	Ottawa	W Parker
Camden East	Midland	S Clarke
Canboro'	Niagara	William Fitch
Cape Cove	Gaspe	Wm Tilly
Cap Sante	Quebec	Geo A Allsopp
Carillon	Montreal	Geo Wanless
Carleton	Gaspe	Jos Meagher
Carleton Place	Bathurst	R Bell
Cavan	Newcastle	J Knowlson
Cedars	Montreal	W Waters
Chambly	Do.	W H Dixon
Champlain	Three Rivers	J E Lanouette

Name of Office.	District.	Postmaster.
Chateauguay	Montreal	Geo Burrill
Chatham	Do.	Lemuel Cushing
Chelsea	Do.	Thos B Prentiss
Chinguacousy	Home	Peleg Howland
Chippawa	Niagara	William Hepburne
Churchville	Home	Daniel Perry
Clarenceville	Montreal	C Goodsil
Clarendon	Do.	J McFarlane
Clarke	Newcastle	John Beavis
Clearville	Western	David H Gesner
Coaticook	Montreal	H Cutting
Cobourg	Newcastle	Thos Scott
Colborne	Do.	J A Keeler
Colchester	Western	Gordon Buchanan
Coldwater	Simcoe	Edmund Moon
Compton	St. Francis	A W Kendrick
Consecon	Prince Edward	W Kirkland
Cooksville	Home	Francis B Morley
Cornwall	Eastern	G C Wood
Coteau du Lac	Montreal	Flora Maguire
Cowansville	Do.	Peter Cowan
Credit	Home	James Magrath
Crowland	Niagara	Wm Vanalstine
Cross Point	Gaspe	John Frazer
Calumet Island	On the Up'r Ottawa	Louis Brissard
Daillebout	Montreal	Robt Turner
Danville	St. Francis	T C Allis
Darlington	Newcastle	R Fairbairn
Dawn Mills	Western	James Smith
Delaware	London	John Drake
Demorestville	Prince Edward	N Sprague
Dereham	Brock	John Simpson Scott
Deschambault	Quebec	F Hamelin
Dewittville	Montreal	J Davidson
Dickinson's Landing	Eastern	W Colquhoun
Drummondville	Niagara	Saml Falconbridge
Drummondville	Three Rivers	J Millar

Name of Office.	District.	Postmaster.
Dundas	Gore	James Bell Ewart
Dundee	Montreal	D Baker
Dunham	Do.	Ed Baker
Dunnville	Niagara	John Armour
Durham	Three Rivers	Robert More
Dudswell	St. Francis	Z Evans
East Farnham	Montreal	Samuel Wood
Eaton	St Francis	Joshua Toss
Edwardsburg	Johnstown	W S Akin
Ekfrid	London	James McIntyre
Eldon	Colborne	Angus Kay
Elora	Wellington	James Ross
Embro'	Brock	Donald Matheson
Emily	Colborne	Robt Grundy
Eramosa	Wellington	George Forster
Erieus	Western	James W Little
Erin	Wellington	William Cornach
Errol	Western	Thomas Laing
Esquesing	Gore	Richard Tracy
Etobicoke	Home	William Gamble
East Oxford	Brock	William Bennett
Easton's Corners	Johnstown	S S Easton
Farmersville	Johnstown	R Giles
Fenelon Falls	Colborne	W Powles
Fergus	Wellington	James McQueen
Fingal	London	Levi Fowler
Finch	Eastern	Adam Cockburn
Fitzroy Harbour	Bathurst	Geo. Learmouth
Flos	Simcoe	John Craig
Fort Erie	Niagara	William Rainsford
Frampton	Quebec	John Ross
Frankford	Midland	Wm Bowen
Franktown	Bathurst	Ewen McEwen
Fredericksburg	Midland	E Sills
Frelighsburg	Montreal	L. Kemp
Frost Village	Do.	H S Foster
Galt	Gore	Absalom Shade

Name of Office.	District.	Postmaster.
Gananoque	Johnstown	J McDonald
Gaspe Basin	Gaspe	John Eden
Gentilly	Three Rivers	Adolphus Stein
Georgeville	Montreal	Chauncey Bullock
Georgina	Home	J O'Brien Bourchier
Gloucester	Ottawa	J Freeman
Goderich	Huron	Thomas Kydd
Gosfield	Western	Josiah Strong
Granby	Montreal	H Lyman
Grenville	Montreal	E Pridham
Grimsby	Niagara	R. F. Nelles
Guelph	Wellington	Robert Corbett
Glandford	Gore	E Bingham
Haldimand	Newcastle	John Taylor
Hamilton	Gore	Edmund Ritchie
Hatley	St. Francis	W G Cook
Hawkesbury	Ottawa	C Hersey
Henryville	Montreal	Horace Wells
Hemmingford	Do.	J Scriver
Hillier	Prince Edward	Philip Flagler
Holland Landing	Simcoe	Wm Jas Sloane
Howard	Western	Duncan Warren
Hull	Montreal	J Anderson
Humber	Home	Robert Bowman
Huntingdon	Montreal	J Robinson
Huntley	Bathurst	John Graham
Hornby	Home	Wm McKindsay
Houghton	Talbot	Benijah M Brown
Hungerford	Victoria	Jas G Downing
Heck's Corners	Johnstown	J S Archibald
Hinchinbrook	Montreal	Jos Holbrook
Indiana	Niagara	Richard Brown
Industry	Montreal	P C Loedel
Innisfil	Simcoe	Benj Ross
Inverness	Quebec	Jos Redfern
Isle-aux Noix	Montreal	Geo Gunn
Isle Verte	Quebec	L Bertrand

Name of Office.	District.	Postmaster.
Jordan	Niagara	William Bradt
Kamouraska	Quebec	Alexis Gagui
Katesville	London	Richard Browne
Kemptville	Johnstown	W H Bottum
Keswick	Home	Cephas Goode
Kilmarnock	Johnstown	J Maitland
King	Home	Donald McCallum
Kingsey	Three Rivers	James W. Wilson
Kitley	Johnstown	Alex. McLean
Kingston	Midland	Robert Deacon
Labaie du Febvre	Three Rivers	J Duguay
LaBeauce	Quebec	J N Chasse
L'Acadie	Montreal	Noel Darche
Lachine	Do.	Jno England
Lachute	Do.	Jno Meikle
Lacolle	Do.	Traver Vanvliet
La Guerre	Do.	Jno McDonald
Lanark	Bathurst	Jno Hall
Lancaster	Eastern	K McPherson
Laprairie	Montreal	J Charlton
L'Assomption	Montreal	J Gilbault
Leeds	Quebec	J N Jiggins
Lennoxville	St Francis	J P Cushing
Les Eboulemens	Quebec	E Slevin
Lindsay	Colborne	David Culbert
L'Islet	Quebec	D S Ballantyne
Litchfield	Montreal	Hiram Cotton
Lloydtown	Home	Anthony Eastwood
Lochaber	Montreal	S B Whitcomb
Lochiel	Eastern	Angus McPhee
London	London	Geo J Goodhue
Longueuil	Montreal	Joseph Lecour
L'Orignal	Ottawa	T H Johnson
Lotbiniere	Quebec	Joseph Fitteau
Loughboro'	Midland	Hugh Madden
Louisville	Western	John Crow
La-cloche	(Lake Huron,)	A W Buchanan

Name of Office.	District.	Postmaster.
McGillivray	Huron	Isaac Moody
McKillop	Do.	George Gouinlock
McNab	Bathurst	James Morris
Madoc	Midland	James McDonell
Maitland	Johnstown	Robert Hervey
Manningville	Montreal	F Ames
Mara	Simcoe	Michael McDonagh
March	Bathurst	Thos Read
Markham	Home	Arch Barker
Mariposa	Colborne	Geo Douglas
Marmora	Midland	J Fidlar
Marshville	Niagara	Edward Lee
Martintown	Eastern	A M'Martin
Maskinonge	Three Rivers	G Saucier
Matilda	Eastern	George Brouse
Melbourne	St Francis	Thos Tait
Merrickville	Johnstown	E H Whitmarsh
Mersea	Western	F A Ambridge
Metis	Quebec	Henry Page
Middleton	Talbot	Joseph Lawson
Milford	Prince Edward	Thos Cook
Milton	Gore	Mathias Teetzel
Mill Creek	Midland	P S Zimmerman
Mohawk	Gore	Abraham Cook
Mono Mills	Simcoe	A Lewis
Montreal	Montreal	James Porteous
Moira	Victoria	W Mullet
Moore	Western	James Baby
Mosa	London	Robt L Warren
Moulinette	Eastern	Thos McCosh
Mulmur	Simcoe	John Little
Murray	Newcastle	Chas Biggar
Murray Bay	Quebec	Cleophe Cimon
Mascouche	Montreal	Philip Mount
Millbrook	Home	M Knowlson
Mount Johnson	Montreal	T Lesage
Monaghan (South)		Jno Clemesha

Name of Office.	District.	Postmaster.
Manitowaning	(On Lake Huron)	
Mac's Corners	Eastern	
Nanticoke	Niagara	Lawrence W Mener
Napanee	Midland	A Campbell
Napierville	Montreal	Loop Odell
Nassagiweya	Gore	Thos Easterbrook
Nelson	Do.	Timothy Cooper
Newboro	Johnstown	Benjamin Tett
New Carlisle	Gaspe	Henry Caldwell
New Glasgow	Montreal	John Lloyd
New Ireland	Quebec	R C Porter
Newmarket	Home	William Roe
Niagara	Niagara	Alex. Davidson
Nicolet	Three Rivers	L M Cressi
North Augusta	Johnstown	S J Bellamy
North Georgetown	Montreal	Benjamin Reeves
North Port	Prince Edward	Samuel Solmes
Norton Creek	Montreal	T Cantwell
Norval	Gore	Wm Clay
Norwich	Brock	Thomas Wallace
Nottawasaga	Simcoe	Angus Campbell
Normandale	Talbot	John Tolmire
Norwood	Colborne	James Foley
North Lancaster	Eastern	Charles Leclair
Newburg	Midland	H G Spafford
Newcastle	Newcastle	John Short
Oakland	Brock	John Toyne
Oakville	Gore	R K Chisholm
Onslow	Montreal	Adam Lindsay
Orillia	Simcoe	William Lloyd
Ormstown	Montreal	Robt Cross
Oro	Simcoe	Edward Ryall
Osgoode	Ottawa	Daniel Cameron
Osnabruck	Eastern	John Bockus
Otanabee	Colborne	Thomas Carr
Otterville	Brock	John H Cornell
Oxford	Brock	James Ingersoll

Name of Office.	District.	Postmaster.
Owen's Sound	Wellington	George Brown
Oshawa	Huron	Edward Skae
Pakenham	Bathurst	A Dickson
Palermo	Gore	Henry M Switzer
Paris	Do.	George Macartney
Pelham	Niagara	John Smith Price
Penetanguishene	Simcoe	W B Hamilton
Pembroke	Bathurst	A Moffatt
Percy	Newcastle	A S Platt
Perth	Bathurst	James Allen
Perce	Gaspe	William Annett
Peterboro	Colborne	S J Carver
Petite Nation	Montreal	D B Papineau
Philipsburg	Do.	W W Smith
Pickering	Home	F Leys
Pike River	Montreal	Abel L Taylor
Picton	Prince Edward	William Rorke
Plantagenet	Ottawa	P McMartin
Point Abino	Niagara	Thomas Disher
Point a Cavagnol	Montreal	P F C Delesderniers
Point St. Peter	Gaspe	John Clark
Port Burwell	London	Leonidas Burwell
Port Colborne	Niagara	Thomas Parke
Port Credit	Home	James Cotton
Port Dalhousie	Niagara	Nathan Pawling
Port Dover	Talbot	Henry Waters
Port Hope	Newcastle	David Smart
Port Maitland	Niagara	Joshua Manly
Portneuf	Quebec	A Gandrie
Port Robinson	Niagara	Duncan McFarland
Port St. Francis	Three Rivers	Smith Leith
Port Sarnia	Western	George Durand
Port Stanley	London	John Bostwick
Port Talbot	Do.	Hannibal Burwell
Portland	Johnstown	P Cole
Pointe Claire	Montreal	P C Valois
Prescott	Johnstown	A Jones

Name of Office.	District.	Postmaster.
Preston	Wellington	Jacob Hespeler
Princeton	Brock	John Thompson
Petersburg	Wellington	John Ernst
Port Rowan	Talbot	A McLennan
Port Daniel	Gaspe	
Quebec	Quebec	John Sewell,
Queenstown	Niagara	John Stayner
Rainham	Do.	Charles Williams
Raleigh	Western	James Read
Ramsay	Bathurst	James Wylie
Rawdon	Victoria	Wm Judd
Rawdon	Montreal	Luke Daly
Reach	Home	Abner Hurd
Richmond	Bathurst	W R R Lyon
Richmond	St. Francis	G K Foster
Richmond Hill	Home	John Wallington
Rigaud	Montreal	S Townier
Rimouski	Quebec	P Ganvreau
Riviere du Loup	Three Rivers	Leon Caron
Riv. du Loup en bas	Quebec	H Davidson
Riviere Ouelle	Do.	C H Tetu
Robinson	St. Francis	Lemuel Pope
Romney	Western	Thomas Renwick
Russelltown	Montreal	John Costello
River Trent	Victoria	James Cummings
Rednersville	Prince Edward	W A Johnson
St. Joseph's	(On Lake Huron)	
Sault Ste. Marie	(Lake Superior)	John Ballenden
St. Andre	Quebec	E Michaud
St. Andrews	Eastern	John Harrison
St. Andrews	Montreal	W G Blanchard
Ste. Anne de la Perade	Three Rivers	Elzear Methot
Ste Anne la Pocatiere	Quebec	D S Marquis
Ste. Anne bout de L'Isle	Montreal	Edw McNaughton

Name of Office.	District.	Postmaster.
St. Antoine	Quebec	Ed Bouchard
St. Benoit	Montreal	F H Lemoine
St. Catharines	Niagara	J P Merritt
St. Cesaire	Montreal	P H Plamondon
St. Charles	Do.	W Lanigan
St. Croix	Quebec	Moses Couture
St. Denis	Montreal	O Chamard
St. Elizabeth	Do.	A B Lafreniere
St. Eustache	Do.	D Mitchell
St. Francis	Three Rivers	J Gill
St. George	Gore	George Stanton
St. Hyacinthe	Montreal	Wm Honey
St. Jacques	Do.	Aime Dugas
St. Jean Pt. Joli	Quebec	J. Michaud
St. Johns	Niagara	John Davis
St. Johns	Montreal	Curtis Pattee
St. Laurent	Do.	D McDonald
St. Luce	Quebec	A E Gauvreau
St. Marie de Monoir	Montreal	F H Gatien
St Jean desChaillons	Quebec	
St. Martin	Montreal	Charles Smallwood
St. Martine	Do.	M A Primeau
St. Ours	Do.	J. Dorion
St. Paul's Bay	Quebec	John Kane
St. Pie	Montreal	George Bridgeman
StPierre lesBecquets	Three Rivers	Alex. Miller
St. Roch L'Achigan	Montreal	Louis Archambault
St. Scholastique	Do.	Wm Snowdon
St. Stanislaus	Three Rivers	B Roy
St. Sylvester	Quebec	Ignace Gagnon
Ste. Therese de Blainville	Montreal	John Morris
St. Thomas	London	E. Ermatinger
St. Thomas	Quebec	Albert Bender
St. Vincent	Simcoe	W Stephenson
St. Vincent de Paul	Montreal	Cesaire Germain
Sandwich	Western	P H Morin

Name of Office.	District.	Postmaster.
Scarboro'	Home	Allan Maclean
Seneca	Niagara	James Little
Seymour East	Newcastle	David Allan
Seymour West	Do.	John Gibb
Shannonville	Victoria	Ronald McMichael
Sharon	Home	John C Hogaboom
Sheffield	Gore	Samuel Congo
Sherbrooke	St. Francis	Wm Brooks
Simcoe	Talbot	Duncan Campbell
Smiths Falls	Johnstown	P Robertson
Smithville	Niagara	W Forsyth
South Pottoh	Montreal	James Manson
South Gower	Johnstown	Wm Bower
Sparta	London	Duncan Wilson
Stanbridge East	Montreal	Z Cornell
Stanley's Mills	Home	Thos Brown Philips
Stanstead	Montreal	P Hubbard
Stoney Creek	Niagara	John Williamson
Stevensville	Do.	Wm Powell
South Monaghan	Newcastle	J Clemisha
Stouffville	Home	John Boyer
Stratford	Huron	John C W Daly
Streetsville	Home	Wm H Patterson
Stukely	Montreal	S Godard
Sunnidale	Simcoe	Alex Gillespie
Sutton	Montreal	Geo C Dyer
Sandhill	Home	Saml Boyer Sterne
Spencersville	Johnstown	W Hopkins
St. Renie	Montreal	T Metras
St. Gervais	Quebec	E M McKenzie
St. Lin	Montreal	Carolus Lauzier
St. Jerome	Do.	A B Lavallie
St. Joseph	Quebec	J O C Arcaud
St. Francois	Do.	F X Pousant
Ste. Brigide	Montreal	James Reid
St. Giles	Quebec	George Cote
St. Roch des Annais	Do.	A Morin

Name of Office.	District.	Postmaster.
St. Simon	Three Rivers	F X Cadieux
St. Hugues	Do.	J B Langlois
St. Aime	Do.	J Durocher
St. Polycarpe	Montreal	Jno Taylor
Storrington	Midland	Hugh Spring
St. Mathias	Montreal	F Franchere
St. Edouard	Do.	T Beaudin
St. Henri	Quebec	J B Carrier
St. Barthelemi	Montreal	Fras Rouleau
St. Raphaels	Eastern	D F McDonell
Tecumseh	Simcoe	David Evans
Terrebonne	Montreal	A McKenzie
Thamesville	Western	Nathan Cornwall
Thornhill	Home	William Parsons
Thorold	Niagara	Peter Keefer
Three Rivers	Three Rivers	Jno Robertson
Toronto City	Home	Charles Berczy
Tralalgar	Gore	Alex Proudfoot
Trois Pistoles	Quebec	Felix Tetu
Tuckersmith	Huron	Richard Thwaite
Tyrconnell	London	Leslie Patterson
Uxbridge	Home	Jos Bascom
Vankleekhill	Ottawa	Neil Stewart
Varennes	Montreal	Eugene Talham
Vaudreuil	Do.	J O Bastim
Vaughan	Home	George Stegman
Vercheres	Montreal	F X Collette
Vienna	London	Wm B Wrong
Vittoria	Talbot	Simpson McCall
Wallaceburgh	Western	Calvin Smith
Walpole	Niagara	W Barker
Walsingham	Talbot	Hardinge G King
Waterford	Do.	James Loder Green
Warwick	Western	C R Nixon
Waterdown	Gore	Robert Lottridge
Waterloo	Montreal	H Robinson
Waterloo	Wellington	Daniel Snyder

Name of Office.	District.	Postmaster.
Welland Port	Niagara	Luke Cavers
Wellington	Prince Edward	A McFaul
Wellington Square	Gore	Hiram Smith
West Flamboro	Do.	Walter Colcleuch
Westmeath	Bathurst	C S Bellows
West Shefford	Montreal	A McKenny
Whitby	Home	A McPherson
Williamsburg East	Eastern	M Pillar
Williamsburg North	Do.	Walter Bell
Willamsburg West	Do.	James Holden
William Henry	Montreal	E L Hayden
Williamstown	Eastern	D McNicol
Wilmot	Wellington	Robert Hays
Winchester	Eastern	G Armstrong
Wilton	Midland	S Warner
Windsor	Western	John McCrae
Weston	Home	John A Donaldson
Williams	Huron	Donald McIntosh
Woodstock	Brock	H C Barwick
Woolwich	Wellington	James Davidson
Warsaw	Colborne	Thomas Choate
Wolf Island	Midland	Mary Hitchcock
West Huntingdon	Victoria	Philip Luke
West Farnham	Montreal	J F Whitfield
West Port	Johnstown	Aaron Chambers
Yamachiche	Three Rivers	Modeste Richer
Yamaska	Do.	F Hebert
Yonge	Johnstown	J G Leavett
York	Niagara	Alex Scobie
York Mills	Home	C Van Nostrand
Zone Mills	Western	G P Kirby.

APPENDIX

TO THE

CANADIAN MERCANTILE ALMANAC

FOR 1847,

SUPPLIED FROM THE BEST SOURCES,

BY SCOBIE & BALFOUR, TORONTO.

Common Council of the City of Toronto.

Mayor—William Henry Boulton, Esquire, M. P. P.

ST. DAVID'S WARD.

Aldermen—Hon. H. Sherwood, M.P.P.; *Angus Bethune, Esq.
Common Councilmen—Mr. George Platt; *Mr. Samuel Mitchell.

ST. PATRICK'S WARD.

Aldermen—W. H. Boulton, Esq., M.P.P.; *G. T. Denison, jr. Esq.
Common Councilmen—Mr. James Trotter; *Mr. Jonathan Dunn.

ST. ANDREW'S WARD.

Aldermen—J. H. Cameron, Esq. M.P.P; G. Duggan, Esq. M.P.P.
Common Councilmen—Mr. John Ritchey; *Mr. Alex. Macdonald.

ST. LAWRENCE WARD.

Aldermen—J. Beaty, Esq.; *Robert Beard, Esq.
Common Councilmen—Mr. Joshua G. Beard; *Mr. Samuel Platt.

ST. GEORGE'S WARD.

Aldermen—William Wakefield, Esq.; *George Gurnett, Esq.
Common Councilmen—Mr. T. J. Preston; *Mr. John Craig.

The gentlemen marked thus * retire from the Council on the first Monday in February, but may be elected to serve again at the municipal election on the second Tuesday in January.

The days of meeting of the Council are usually Mondays, in the evening. The members of the Common Council are elected by a majority of the registered voters of the City of Toronto. The lists of persons entitled to vote for each Ward are exhibited in the City Hall, from the first Monday in December until the day of the election (the second Tuesday in January). Persons interested should make a point of seeing that their names are not omitted or mis-spelt, as no alterations in such lists can be made unless four day's notice is given in writing to the Clerk of the Common

A

Council of the desire to have any name altered, inserted, or erased, and no one is allowed to vote whose name does not appear on the said lists.

OFFICERS OF THE CORPORATION.

Coroners .... { John King, M. D.
                             { G. Duggan, sen., Esq.
Clerk of the Common Council .... Charles Daly.
Chamberlain .... Andrew T. McCord.
High Bailiff .... G. L. Allen.
City Inspector .... Thomas Garlick.
Clerk of the Market .... Richard Harrison.
Weigh Master and Clerk of the } John Dempsey.
   Fish Market ....

The Eastern Station House is in the City Hall, where two of the police are always on duty, and can be obtained in case of necessity.

Police Constables—James Magarr, Duchess-street; Thomas Kenny, Sumach-street; Jonathan Townsend, Sherborne-street; Wm. Ramsey, Francis-street.

The Western Station House is near the corner of Queen and John-streets, where Constables are also always on duty.

Police Constables—Francis Earls, Richmond-street; Robert Trotter, Station House; Robert Campbell, Queen-street; Andrew Fleming, Queen-street.

Fire Inspector—Robert Alexander.

REGULATIONS FOR CABS.
CAB STANDS.

No. 1, east side of West Market Place.
No. 2, east side of Church-street, between King and Adelaide streets.
No. 3, middle of King-street, west of Macdonald's Hotel.

CITY DIVISIONS, BY WHICH FARES ARE REGULATED.

1st Division, between Simcoe-street on the west, Queen-street on the north, and Parliament-street on the east. 2nd Division, between Simcoe-street and Brock-street on the west, the northern limits of the city on the north, and the River Don on the east. 3rd Division, the remainder of the City and Liberties beyond the last described division. Streets forming boundaries are within the division in which they are first named.

Persons detaining Cabs not more than five minutes at their place of destination, are entitled to return without extra charge. If detained beyond five minutes and under a quarter of an hour, the driver is entitled to one half extra as return fare; if over a quarter and under half an hour, two-thirds; if more than half an hour, it is optional to charge by time. A reasonable weight of luggage allowed, without extra charge.

Fares from any one divison to the adjoining one, to be charged same as from 1st to 2nd division.

Any person calling a cab from its stand, and not employing it, may be charged one half the lowest rate of fare.

SCHEDULE OF FARES.

PLACES.	Coaches, &c. drawn by two horses.				CABS.			
	One Person.	Two Persons.	Three Persons.	Each add'l Person.	One Person.	Two Persons.	Three Persons.	Each add'l Person.
	s. d.	s. d.	s. d.	s. d.	s. d.	s. d.	s. d.	s. d.
From the steamboat landing, or any of the Stands, to any place within the 1st Division, and *vice versa* - -	1 0	1 9	2 3	0 6	0 7½	0 11	1 3	0 3
From the steamboat landing, or any of the Stands, to any place within the 2nd Division, and *vice versa* - -	1 6	2 3	2 9	0 6	0 11	1 3	1 7	0 3½
From the steamboat landing, or any of the Stands, to any place within the 3rd Division, and *vice versa* - -	2 0	2 9	3 3	0 6	1 3	1 9	2 6	0 4
Time per hour	1st hour, 4s.; every subsequent hour, 3s. 1½d.				1st hour, 2s. 6d.; each subsequent hour, 2s.			

Toronto, Hamilton and Niagara Electro-Magnetic Telegraph Company.

CAPITAL £4000.

President—Clarke Gamble, Esq.
Vice President—Thomas G. Ridout, Esq.
Directors — E. F. Whittemore, Daniel McNab, W. B. Jarvis, James Browne, J. L. Ramsey, T. D. Harris, R. Juson.
Secretary—Robert McClure.

The annual meeting is held at Toronto, on the First Monday of October, in each year.

TORONTO BUILDING SOCIETY.

Incorporated by Act of Parliament.

SHARES £100 EACH.

Monthly Subscription, 10s. per share, Entrance Fee, 5s. per share. Transfer Fee, 2s. 6d. per share.

Directors—Hon. S. B. Harrison, President ; T. W. Birchall, Esq., Vice President ; William Botsford Jarvis Esq., William Henry Boulton, Esq., M.P.P., Charles Berczy, Esq., Lewis Moffatt, Esq., Hon. James E. Small.

Secretary and Treasurer—W. C. Ross, Esquire.

Office Wellington Buildings, Church-street, Toronto.

The City of Toronto and Lake Huron Railroad Company.

(INCORPORATED BY ACT OF PARLIAMENT.)

Capital £500,000,—in 100,000 Shares of £5 each.

OFFICE, 168, KING STREET, TORONTO.

President—The Honourable William Allan.

Vice President—George P. Ridout, Esq. (President of the Board of Trade)

Directors—Clarke Gamble, Esq. ; John Ewart, Esq. ; the Hon. Henry Sherwood, M.P.P. ; William H. Boulton, Esq., Mayor of the City of Toronto, M.P.P. ; William Proudfoot, Esq., President of the Bank of Upper Canada ; Frederick Widder, Esq., Commissioner of the Canada Company ; George Ridout, Esq. ; Mr. William Atkinson ; Donald Bethune, Esq.

Secretary pro tem.—Edward George O'Brien, Esq.

Bankers—The Bank of Upper Canada.

City of Toronto & Lake Huron Railroad Company, London.

(*In Connection with the above.*)

Capital £3,500,000.

Under Deed of Settlement, finally registered, agreeably to British Acts of Parliament.

Chairman—Charles Franks, Esq., Governor of the Canada Co.

Deputy Chairman—H. H. Berens, Esq.

Secretary—William Thomas Smith, Esq.

Directors—Pierce S. Butler, Esq., M. P., John Easthope, Lieut. Col. Head, Frederick C. Gaussen, F. H. Mitchell, Edward Seard, Alexander Stewart, William Wilson.

Office—Canada House, St. Helen's Place, Bishopsgate Street.

British America Fire and Life Assurance Company.

Incorporated under an Act of the Third Session of the Eleventh Provincial Parliament of Upper Canada, and empowered under an Act of the Second Session of the First Parliament of Canada, to effect Inland Marine Assurances.

Capital £100,000, *in Shares of* £12 10s. *each.*

Governor—The Honourable William Allan.

Deputy Governor—George Perceval Ridout.

Board of Direction—William Atkinson, Angus Bethune, George Duggan, Junior, Hon. James Gordon, Colonel R. R. Loring, William Proudfoot, Col. Charles B. Turner, Hon. Christopher Widmer, Dr. Burnside, Thos. Brunskill, John Ewart, Thos. Helliwell, Edward McMahon, James M. Strachan, Charles Watkins.

Trustees—John Ewart, William Proudfoot, Dr. Burnside.

Managing Director—Thomas William Birchall.

Solicitor—Clark Gamble.

Bank—The Bank of Upper Canada.

Office—George Street, corner of Duke Street, Toronto.

The Board meets weekly, on Tuesdays, at Eleven o'clock.

Agencies—Montreal, Joseph Wenham ; Kingston, William Craig ; Cobourg, Robert Henry ; Peterboro', W. H. Wrighton ; Whitby, Edward Skae ; Niagara, George Ward ; St. Catharines, George Rykert ; Hamilton, Andrew Steven ; London, William W. Street ; Port Stanley, Richard Smith ; Woodstock, William Lapenotiere ; Chatham, William Cosgrave.

Forms of Proposal and all requisite information may be obtained at the Office of the Company or any of its agencies.

Ætna Fire and Inland Navigation Insurance Company.

HARTFORD, CONNECTICUT.

Toronto Agency—Edward G. O'Brien, Esq.

Office—168 King-street, (corner of Frederick-street.)

Hamilton Agency—W. P. McLaren, Esquire.

National Fire and Life Assurance Company.

Capital—£500,000.

Empowered by Act of Parliament, 2nd Victoria Royal Assent, 27th, July 1838.

Chairman—T. Lambie Murray, Esq. ; *and a London Board of Directors.*

A 3

United States Board of Local Directors—Office, 74 Wall-street—
   Chairman—Jacob Harvey, John J. Palmer, Jonathan Goodhue,
   James Boorman, George Barclay, Samuel S. Howland, Gorham
   A. Worth, Samuel M. Fox, and William Van Hook, Esquires,
   New York ; Clement C. Biddle, Sears C. Walker, Louis A.
   Godey, and George Rex Graham, Esquires, Philadelphia.

General Agent—J. Leander Starr, } *For the United States and*
General Accountant — Edward T.   } *British North American*
   Richardson,   } *Colonies.*

Toronto Board of Local Directors—President—Hon. S. B. Harrison ; Charles C. Small, William Botsford Jarvis, William
   Boulton, M.P.P., Charles Berczy, Lewis Moffatt, Dr. Gwynne
   and Colley Foster, Esquires.

Bankers—Bank of British North America.

Medical Examiner—Doctor Sullivan.

Agents { W. C. Ross, Esq., *Wellington Buildings.*
         { Edward Goldsmith, Esq., *Toronto.*

Applications for Prospectuses, &c., to be made to Mr. Ross, at
the Office of the Society, Wellington Buildings, Toronto.

Home District Mutual Fire Insurance Company.

President—James Harvey Price.

Secretary and Treasurer—John Rains.

Directors—John McMurrich, James Beaty, John Eastwood, James
   Lesslie, Dr. Workman, John Doel, William Mathers, A.
   M‘Master, J. B. Warren, B. W. Smith.

Bank—The Bank of Upper Canada.

Office—Nelson Street, opposite Adelaide Street.

   Amount of Premium Notes on hand · · · · £42,809 15 0
   Amount under Insurance · · · · · · · · · · · · £316,901 0 0

Phœnix Fire Assurance Company.
Lombard-street, London.

Agents for Toronto—Moffatts, Murray & Co.

Britannia Life Assurance Company.
Princess-street, Bank, London.

Insurance effected in this office on lives from 16 years to 70, for
the purpose of securing debts, or a reversionary property, which can
by no other means be acquired.

Capital—One Million Sterling.

Agent in Toronto—F. Lewis, 222 King-street.

Eagle Life Assurance Company.

London—Established by Act of Parliament, 1807.

Chairman—John Richards, Esquire.

Deputy Chairman—Sir James McGrigor, Bart., F. R. S.

Directors—Sir Archer Denman Croft, Bart., Lieut. General Sir J. Wilson, K. C. B., Wm. Augustus Rear Admiral Sir Montague, G. C. H., Chas. Barry Baldwin, Esq., M. P., Charles Thomas Holcombe, Walter Anderson Peacock, Peter Skipper, John Spurgin, M. D., Henry Tufnel, Esq., M. P., Wm. Wybrow.

Auditors—C. J. Campbell, J. G. Lynde, T. G. Sambrooke.

Toronto Agency—Consulting Surgeon, Walter Telfer, Church Street ; Agent, John Cameron, Commercial Bank, from whom forms and all necessary information can be obtained. (Four-fifths of the profits septennially revert to the assured ; the sum thus returned may either be added to the amount of the claim, or immediately applied to diminish the future payments.)

Montreal Fire, Life, and Inland Navigation Assurance Company.

Incorporated by a Special Ordinance, 1840, *and by Provincial Act 6th Victoria*, cap. 22. *Capital*, 200,000.

President—James Ferrier, Esq.

Manager—William Murray, Esq.

Office—Great St. James Street, Montreal.

Agents—J. G. Irvine, Quebec ; R. Watson, Brockville ; John Ross, Bellville ; John Burke, Whitby ; Colin C. Ferrie, Hamilton ; J. L. Ranney, St. Catharines ; W. R. Eckart, Cleveland ; Robert Headlam, Prescott ; John Macaulay, Kingston ; C. H. Morgan, Cobourg ; Robert Beekman, Toronto ; Alex. Davidson, Niagara ; G. R. Williams, Port Stanley ; W. & J. Bell, Perth ; Robert K. Chisholm, Oakville ; M. Stevenson, Bytown. William Roebuck, Salvage Agent, Coteau du Lac ; A. J. Barnhart, Salvage Agent, Barnhart's Island, near Cornwall.

St. Lawrence Inland Marine Assurance Company.

Capital, £100,000.

Agents—C. T. Palsgrave, Montreal ; D. B. O. Ford, Brockville ; R. Deacon, Kingston ; E. Perry, Cobourg ; J. Welsh, Whitby ; C. D. Sheldon, Barnhart Island ; E. Ritchie, Hamilton ; A. K. Boomer, St. Catharines ; William Roebuck, Coteau du Lac ; George Henderson, north-east corner of the Market, Toronto.

A 4

Provincial Agricultural Association and Board of Agriculture for Canada West.

President—E. W. Thomson, Esq.

Vice Presidents—John Wetenhall, Esq., Mr. Sheriff Ruttan.

Secretary and Treasurer—W. G. Edmundson.

Fair to be held at Hamilton, in October, 1847.

Committee of Management—Mayor of Toronto, E. W. Thomson, Esq., John Wetenhall, Esq., Mr. Sheriff Ruttan, W. G. Edmundson, Esq., Hon. Adam Ferguson, Mr. Sheriff Jarvis, Colonel Burrowes, Franklin Jackes, Esq., William Thompson, Esq., J. B. Ewart, Esq., David Smart, Esq.

Union Agricultural Society of Thorah, Brock, Georgina and North Gwillimbury.

Instituted in 1845.—*Annual subscription five shillings.*

President—Colonel Kenneth Cameron.

Treasurer—William Bourchier, Esquire.

Secretary—Charles Sibbald, Esquire.

CANADA COMPANY.

Incorporated by Act of Parliament and Royal Charter, 1826. *Capital* £1,000,000 *sterling, with power to increase it to* £2,000,000 *sterling.*

Office in London—Canada House, St. Helen's Place, Bishopsgate Street. *Offices in Canada*—Toronto, Frederick Street, and Goderich, Huron District.

Commissioners resident in Canada West—Thomas Mercer Jones, and Frederick Widder.

Any information respecting the Company's Land can be also obtained from Richard Birdsall, Asphodel, Colborne District ; Dr. Alling, Guelph, Wellington District ; and J. C. W. Daly, Stratford, Huron District.

The Canada Company have for sale about 800,000 acres in the Huron District, and 800,000 acres in blocks and scattered lots in every township in Canada West.

The Canada Company remit from London to Canada any sum of money by letters of credit upon their Commissioners, and likewise transmit any sum of money from Canada to any part of Europe, by letters of credit upon the Directors.

Bank of Upper Canada, Toronto.

Capital £500,000.

BOARD OF DIRECTORS.

President—Wm. Proudfoot. *Vice-President*—Hon. Christopher Widmer. Angus Bethune, William Cayley, T. C. Street, Francis M. Cayley, James G. Chewett, Wm. Gamble, Samuel P. Jarvis, Thomas Helliwell, Francis Boyd, Joseph Ridout R. R. Loring, Hon. Captain Baldwin, R.N.

Discount Day—Wednesday.

Cashier—Thomas G. Ridout.

OFFICES AND AGENCIES.

Montreal—Joseph Wenham.	*St. Catharines*—Alfred Stow.
Bytown—Thomas J. Leggatt.	*London*—James Hamilton.
Kingston—William G. Hinds.	*Chatham*—William Cosgrove.
Port Hope—Elias P. Smith.	*Goderich*—John McDonald.
Niagara—Thomas McCormick.	*Barrie*—John Moberly.

FOREIGN AGENTS.

New York—Messrs. Prime, Ward & King. *London*—Messrs. Glyn, Hallifax, Mills & Co.; Messrs. Coutts & Co.; Messrs. Barclay, Beven, Tritton & Co.; Messrs. Herries, Farquhar & Co. *Scotland*—British Linen Company Bank at Edinburgh, and all its branches.

Commercial Bank of the Midland District, Kingston.

Capital £500,000.

Incorporated by Act of the Provincial Parliament.

President.—Hon. John Hamilton.

Vice-President.—Hon. John Kirby.

Directors—R. S. Aitcheson, Joseph Bruce, William Logie, John A. Macdonald, M.P.P.; John McPherson, Hon. John Macaulay, James Nickalls, Douglass Prentiss.

Cashier—Francis A. Harper. *Inspector*—Alexander Campbell. *Teller*—Christopher Ede. *Book-keeper*—William F. Harper. *Discount Clerk*—Joseph Rorke. *Assistant do.*—Andrew Drummond, Jr. *Clerk*—John R. Monro. *Messenger*—Wm. Logie. *Solicitors*—John A. Macdonald & Campbell.

Discount Days—Mondays and Thursdays.

BRANCHES AND AGENCIES.

Toronto—John Cameron, Cashier; James S. Thomson, Accountant; James G. Harper, Teller; Archibald Cameron, Discount Clerk; William Pyper, Book-keeper; Robert D. O'Brien, Messenger; Strachan & Cameron, Solicitors. Discounts daily.

A 5

Montreal—Charles S. Ross, Cashier; Charles J. Campbell, Teller; —— McDougal, Book-keeper; Thomas S. Shortt, Messenger; W. Ross, Solicitor. Discounts daily.

Hamilton—Henry McKinstry, Cashier; T. C. Simons, Teller; A. Roxburgh, Messenger; Sir A. N. MacNab & Harvey, Solicitors. Discounts daily.

Cobourg—Redford C. Robins, Cashier; —— Ruthven, Clerk; Solicitor, Donald Bethune, Jr. Discounts daily.

Brockville—Hon. James Morris, Cashier; Robert Findlay, Teller; George Sherwood, Solicitor. Discounts daily.

Bytown—Andrew Drummond, Cashier; Augustus Keefer, Solicitor. Discounts daily.

Belleville—John Turnbull, Agent. *Galt*—Adam Ainslie, Agent. *Holland Landing*—Arthur McMaster, Agent. *London*—Charles Monsarrat, Agent. *Oshawa*—James Laing, Agent. *Picton*—David Smith, Agent. *Port Stanley*—G. R. Williams, Agent. *St. Catharines*—George Rykert, Agent.

England—London Joint Stock Bank, London. *Scotland*—Commercial Bank of Scotland, Edinburgh, and all its branches and agencies in Scotland; Clydesdale Bank, Glasgow, and offices. *Ireland*—Boyle, Low, Pim & Co., Dublin. *New York*—David S. Kennedy.

At all of the above, deposits can be made by parties emigrating to Canada, or those who have friends resident in Canada, for which letters of credit will be issued, and which will be paid with the highest rate of Exchange, at the Commercial Bank, Kingston, or any of its branches, offices, or agencies, on presentation.

BANK OF MONTREAL.

President—The Honorable Peter McGill.
Vice President—The Honorable Joseph Masson.

Directors—T. B. Anderson, Harrison Stephens, John Torrance, James Logan, William Lunn, John Brooke, Joseph Shuter, John Fry, John Molson, John Redpath, and William Molson.

LIST OF OFFICERS.

Montreal—Alexander Simpson, Cashier; William Gunn, Assistant Cashier; Joseph Webster, Accountant; James F. Smith, Assistant Accountant; John Porteous, Second Accountant; Robert Spens, Third Accountant; Francis M. Holmes, First Teller; John G. Horne, Second Teller; C. J. Brown, Third Teller; John Lloyd, Discount Clerk; John G. Adams, Clerk; George A. Holmes, Clerk; David Scott, Clerk; Charles Miller, Clerk; H. B. Picken, Messenger; James Brennan, Porter.

Quebec Branch—James Bolton, Cashier ; H. Legge, Accountant ;
J. Meiklejohn, First Teller ; C. H. Gates, Second Teller; Philip
Lisner, Discount Clerk ; W. Martin, Messenger.

Toronto Branch—William Wilson, Cashier ; James Keiller, Accountant ; W. P. Street, Teller ; W. G. Telfer, Discount
Clerk ; Quinton McNider, Clerk.

Brockville—James Stevenson, Agent ; R. H. Street, Clerk.

Kingston—Colin Miller, Agent; George Dyett, Accountant; G. M.
Yarwood, Teller ; James Gray, Clerk ; R. Richardson, Clerk.

Cobourg—Charles H. Morgan, Agent ; Thomas Lee, Accountant ;
A. C. Hammond, Clerk.

Hamilton—Hugh C. Baker, Agent : P. Stevenson, Accountant ;
Robert Ferrie, Teller ; Frederick G. Holmes, Clerk.

Guelph—Dr. Alling, Agent.

St. Catherines—H. Mittleberger, Agent; H. J. Hensleigh, Clerk.

London—John Fraser, Agent ; W. W. Street, Accountant ; J.
Scott, Clerk.

Bytown—W. H. Hopper, Agent ; M. Stevenson, Clerk.

Port Stanley—Richard Smith, Agent.

St. Thomas—E. Ermatinger, Agent.

Belleville—Philip Ham, Agent.

Picton—William Rorke, Agent.

Cornwall—William Mattice, Agent.

Peterboro'—R. Nicholls, Agent.

Windsor and Amherstburgh—Messrs. J. and J. Dougall, Agents.

AGENTS IN GREAT BRITAIN.

London—Messrs. Glyn, Halifax, Mills & Co.

Liverpool—The Bank of Liverpool.

Edinburgh—British Linen Company and Branches.

AGENTS IN NOVA SCOTIA AND NEW BRUNSWICK.

Halifax—Bank of Nova Scotia.

St. John—Commercial Bank New Brunswick.

AGENTS IN THE UNITED STATES.

New York—D. S. Kennedy.

Boston—Samuel Henshaw & Son.

BANK OF BRITISH NORTH AMERICA.

Established in 1836—Incorporated by Royal Charter in 1840.

Directors—Henry Barnewall, Robert Brown, Sir Robert Campbell,
Bart., Robert Carter, William Chapman, William R. Chapman,
James John Cummins, James Dowie, Oliver Farrer, Alex'r.
Gillespie, Junr., Sir A. Pellet Green, R. N., G. R. Robinson.

A 6

Secretary—George De Bosco Attwood.
Inspector of Branches—Thomas Paton.

BRANCHES.

Quebec—Robert Cassels, Manager. *Montreal*—David Davidson, Manager. *Toronto* — Lewis Moffat and Charles Berczy, Local Directors; Walter Cassels, Manager. (Discount Days —Tuesday and Friday, at 10 A. M.) *Kingston*—Thomas Askew, Manager. *Hamilton*—John Jaffray, Manager. *Port Hope*—David Smart, Agent. *Bytown*—James MacKinnon, Agent. *Dundas*—J. B. Ewart, Agent. *Halifax, Nova Scotia*—S. N. Binney, Manager. *St. John, New-Brunswick*— Alfred Smithers, Manager. *Fredericton, New-Brunswick*— Geo. Taylor Manager. *St. John's, Newfoundland*—A. Milroy, Manager.

London—Glyn, Halifax, Mills & Co. *New-York*—Bell, Maclachlan & Ransom.

GORE BANK, HAMILTON.

Incorporated by Act of the Provincial Parliament.
Capital—£100,000.

Directors—Colin C. Ferrie, John Davidson, Hon. Adam Ferguson, Robert Riddell, Thomas C. Street, Edward Jackson, David Thompson, James Gage, Richard Martin, Robert Pitt Brown.

President—Colin C. Ferrie.   *Cashier*—Andrew Steven.
Teller—Richard P. Street.   *Book Keeper*—Francis Kennedy.
Discount Clerk—Wm. Griffin.   *Clerk*—William Henry Parke.

Discount Day—Tuesday in each week.

AGENTS.

Simcoe—Duncan Campbell. *Woodstock*—H. C. Barwick. *London* —Samuel Read. *Galt*—Absalom Shade. *Guelph*—Thomas Sandilands. *Beamsville*—John B. Osborne. *Brantford*— John A. Wilkes & Sons. *St. Thomas*—Hope & Hodge. *Chatham*—Witherspoon and Charteris.

Toronto—The Bank of Upper Canada, and all its Agents in Canada, where the Gore Bank has no Agents.

England—London—Reid, Irving & Co.; Barclay, Bevan, Tritton & Co.; Coutts & Co.; Curries & Co.; Smith, Payne & Smiths. *Liverpool*—Reid, Irving & Co.; and the Manchester and Liverpool Bank and its branches.

Scotland—Edinburgh—The Bank of Scotland and its branches. *Glasgow*—The Union Bank of Scotland and its branches.

Ireland—The Branches of the Provincial Bank of Ireland.
New-York—John Ward & Co. *Rochester*—The Rochester Bank.

CUSTOM OFFICERS, C. W.

TORONTO.

Collector ···················Robert Stanton.
Surveyor ···················John Roy.
First Landing Waiter ········John Hemphill.
Second Landing Waiter········Thomas Watkins.
First Clerk ···············George Graham.
Second Clerk ···············W. R. Gowan.
Housekeeper and Messenger ····W. McKay.

HAMILTON.

Collector···················John Davidson.
Surveyor ···················John Davis.
Landing Waiter ···············Captain Palmer.
Clerk ·····················John Valance.

KINGSTON.

Collector························——— ———.
Surveyor ·····················G. A. Mailleau.
First Landing Waiter·········D. Lynch.
Second Landing Waiter ·······P. Carborough.
Clerk ·······················——— Gowan.

COBOURG.

Collector······· ···········R. Kitson.
Surveyor and Landing Waiter··A. Bertram.

PORT HOPE.

Surveyor ···················——— Whitehead.

DARLINGTON.

Collector···················——— Clark.
Surveyor and Landing Waiter··——— Mitchell.

WINDSOR HARBOUR.

Collector ···················——— Warren.
Landing Waiter ···············Wellesley Ritchie.

OAKVILLE.

Collector····················——— Chisholm.
Surveyor and Landing Waiter··A. Dixon.

PORT CREDIT.

Landing Waiter···············——— Adams.

A 7

LUNATIC ASYLUM, TORONTO.

Medical Superintendent ········ Dr. Walter Telfer.
Warden and Steward ········· R. Cronyn.
Matron ····················· Mrs. Cronyn.
Assistant Surgeon ··········· John Cronyn.

Five Nurses. Seven Keepers.

Commissioners for Erecting Provincial Lunatic Asylum.

Chairman.—W. H. Boulton, Esquire, M. P.P.

The Hon. the Vice Chancellor,
The Hon. Christopher Widmer,
James Grant Chewett, Esquire,
William P. Jarvis, Esquire,
W. B. Beaumont, Esquire.

The Hon. H. H. Killaly,
The Hon. H. Sherwood,
John Ewart, Esquire,
John King, M. D.

Architect.—J. G Howard. *Secretary.*—Charles Daly.

CROWN OFFICE, TORONTO.

Clerk of the Crown and Pleas ·· Charles C. Small,
Deputy Clerk of the Crown ····· John Radenhurst.
First Clerk ···················· William H. Coxwell,
Second Clerk ·················· John Dempsey,
Third Clerk ··················· Thomas Coxwell,
Fourth Clerk ·················· Robert Pearson.
Messenger ····················· John Alexander.

Commissioners Appointed to Enquire into the State, &c., of the Crown Lands Department.

Honourable D. B. Papineau, Honourable William Morris, and James Henderson.

Commissioners Appointed to Enquire into the State, Management, &c., of the Board of Works.

Hon. William Cayley, Hon. F. A. Quesnel, George Sherwood, Moses Judah Hays, and John Redpath.

Commissioners for Investigating Losses Incurred during the Late Rebellion and Invasion.

Western District—John Harris, John Prince, Robert Mercer.
London District—John Harris, John Wilson, Lawrence Lawrason.
Brock District—John Harris, John Arnold, Roger R. Hunter.
Gore District—George Rykert, Edmund Ritchie, John O. Hatt.

Niagara District—Geo. Rykert, Thos. C. Street, P. Delatre.
Simcoe District—Geo. Rykert, Henry Fry, James Dallas.
Johnstown District—Wm. Freeling, Paul Glasford, G. Crawford.
Home District—Geo. Rykert, J. G. Chewett, E. W. Thompson.

Resident District Agents for the Sale of Public Lands.

Western District ············· Patrick McMullen,
Niagara District ············· James. H. Cummings,
Ottawa District ············· Henry W. McCann,
Colborne District ············· Frederick Ferguson,
Wellington District ············· Andrew Geddes,
Eastern District ············· Samuel Hart,
Home District ············· Thomas Baines,
Dalhousie District ············· John Durie,
Victoria District ············· F. McAnnany,
Gore District ············· Peter Carroll,
London District ············· John B. Askin,
Midland District ············· Allan Macpherson,
Brock District ············· John Carroll,
Simcoe District ············· John Alexander.

Commissioners for taking Affidavits, &c., in the Court of Queen's Bench.

HOME DISTRICT.

Donald Bethune, Charles C. Small, James E. Small, George S. Boulton, W. B. Robinson, John Scott, William Parsons, John F. Taylor, John Warren, Edward Goldsmith, Thomas H. Taylor, W. H. Draper, John G. Spragge, C. B. Secord, W. A. Campbell, George Lount, F. S. Jarvis, John Ridout, W. H. Coxwell, R. B. Sullivan, Clarke Gamble, Michael Burrett, James H. Price, John Powell, John Carey, Angus Bethune, James McGrath, Jr., Alex. Grant, Wm. H. Boulton, George Walton, John Embleton, Charles Magrath, Henry W. Blackstone, Colley Foster, Allan Cameron, Henry Baldwin, Jr., Wm. B. Heward, Wm. H. Blake, John S. Smith, James M. Strachan, Joseph C. Morrison, Robert E. Burns, John H. Cameron, John Moore, Augustus B. Sullivan, R. P. Crooks, George T. Dennison, Jr., Adam Wilson, George D. Wells, Wm. D. Powell, Wm. C. Keele, Secker Brough, Sidney M. Sanford, John H. Hagarty, John Crawford, Henry Eccles, S. B. Fairbanks, Walter Mackenzie, John Hector, John Radenhurst, W. J. Fitzgerald, W. A. Maingy, George Boomer, Thomas Moore, George A. Philpotts, James F. Saxon, Norman G. Ham, Charles Seymour, Francis M. Keller, Joel T. Robinson, Richard Carney, Thomas

Ewart, George Brock, Stedman B. Campbell, Robert G. Dalton, Archibald G. McLean, John Ford Maddock, John Strathy, Zaccheus Burnham, Oliver Mowat, Thomas S. Groome, Tobias Switzer-Walton D. Walton, Skeffington Connor, Angus Morrison, John Lawder, Alexander McPherson, George Brooke, William Stephen, son, John R. Holden, P. M. M. S. Vankoughnet, Douglass Fraser, Frederick T. Wilkes, Samuel B. Harrison, Charles Durand, Bernard F. Ball, Stephen Richards, Jr., Alexander McDonell, Charles W. Cooper, James Daniell, James Lukin Robinson, Ambrose Gorham, Joseph R. Thompson, William Ramsay, Thomas Galt, Richard Dempsey, Daniel G. Miller, Larratt W. Smith, James J. Bell, David B. Reed, G. F. Hughes, John W. Dempsey, William Eccles, James Muttlebury, Alexander Stewart, Edward B. Palmer.

LONDON DISTRICT.

John B. Askin, James Ingersoll, G. W. Whitehead, Edward Ermatinger, W. K. Cornish, John Stuart, John Wilson, John Harris, James Givins, Gideon Ackland, James Hamilton, John Burwell, James Crysler, Ira Scholfield, W. Laponotiere, William Horton, Thomas D. Warren, F. Wright, William D. Powell, John Stewart, Henry C. R. Becher, Thomas Kier, John H. L. Askin, Alexander D. McLean, William Warren Street, James Shanley, Murdoch Mackenzie, Henry Warren, James Daniell, George Williams, John Hutcheson.

NEWCASTLE DISTRICT.

Richard D. Chatterton, David Brodie, Henry Covert, C. M. Boswell, D. E. Boulton, G. S. Boulton, D. Bethune, R. H. Throop, Hon. Z. Burnham, J. Husman, A. H. Meyers, E. Meyers, James Robertson, Joseph Keeler, D. Campbell, George C. Ward, M. F. Whitehead, James Smith, Nisbett Kirchhoffer, William Wallace, Elias Burnham, Stafford Kirkpatrick, James Armour, John W. Love, Thomas V. Murphey, David Culvert, John Scott, Robert Fairburn, William Cottingham, Charles Knowlson, Jr., John Knowlson, John Hewson, George B. Hall, Alfred Rubidge, Henry S. Reid, John Brooks Crowe, Donald Bethune, Jr., Robert M. Boucher, James Marshall Brodie, Norman G. Ham, Archibald Macdonald, Sidney Smith, W. A. Garrett, R. J. Everitt, B. F. Ewing, John H. Hagarty, R. Armour, Zaccheus Burnham, George Eyre Henderson.

BROCK DISTRICT.

W. Lapenotiere, Simon F. Robertson, Thomas S. Short, Edmund Burton, David S. McQueen, Joseph Davis, A. Givins, Hugh C. Darwick, Ira Schofield, Jr., Henry Fenkle, David John Hughes.

OTTAWA DISTRICT.

Peter Freel, William Z. Cozens, Neil Stewart, Thomas H. Johnson, Archibald Macdonell, William K. Mackenzie, George M. Crysler, Walter Bell, Donald Alexander McDonald, Peter O'Brian, Thomas Murphy, James McIntosh, A. J. McMillan, Albert Allsaint Chesley.

GORE DISTRICT.

William A. Maingy, Adam Ainslie, Henry Moyle, Samuel B Freeman, E. W. Secord, David Wall, Douglas Fraser, Hugh B Wilson, George W. Burton, John Smith, Hiram Capron, John Strathy, Thomas Lloyd, William A. Harvey, William D. Powell, John R. Holden, Colin D. Reed, Robert K. Chisholm, Alexander Stewart, Abraham Kenedy Smith.

TALBOT DISTRICT.

John C. Carey, Joseph Davis, William M. Wilson, A. Givens, John H. L. Askin, Henry Warren, Murdoch McKenzie, Francis G. Stanton, William Gundrey.

WESTERN DISTRICT.

William D. Baby, Alexander Duff, Froome Talford, Peter McGlashan, Alexander D. McLean, Joseph Fluett, John Cowan, Robert Reynolds, William Duff, Joseph Taylor, Lionel Johnson, Charles K. Nixon, John G. Wier, J. B. Baby, William Elliott, P. Rapiljei, Alexander Richardson, Alexander Chewitt, James Woods, Charles Askin, John L. Williams, Philip Ham, Kenneth Robertson, William P. Vidal.

JOHNSTOWN DISTRICT.

T. H. Merick, Robert Headlam, Eleazer H. Whitmarsh, Worship Booker McLean, Stephen M. Jarvis.

COLBORNE DISTRICT.

George Green, W. H. Wrighton, Edmund Burton, Jacob Ham, Alfred Rubidge, Robert Armour, Ivan O'Beirne, C. Moe, Henry Baldwin, jun., James Scott.

HURON DISTRICT.

Morgan Mamilton, H. Fraser, John Colville, Watson Dixie.

BATHURST DISTRICT.

John Scott, Terrence H. Merrick, Augustus Keefer, William Oscar Buell, Henry W. Sache, Alexander Moffatt Deacon, George T. Bushe, Charles Bathurst, Thomas M. Radenhurst, Sewel Ormsby, George Lyon, A. Frazer, James Inglis, William Rogerson, Robert Sheriff, Mathew Connell, —— Bell, James Lowe, William McKenzie, Edward Malloch, Charles F. Baines, Daniel McMartin,

A 9

W. P. Lauchs, G. W. Baker, James Bell, Thomas O'Neil, Andrew Dickson, jun.

DALHOUSIE DISTRICT.

Ephraim Jones Hubbell, James Hubbell, John B. Lewis, Robert Hervey, jun., John Scott, Elkanah Billings.

SIMCOE DISTRICT.

Robert B. Miller, Henry W. Blackstone, W. A. Harvey, James R. Gowan, Thomas Lloyd, Thomas Maconchy, Patrick Patton, Andrew Jardine, John Craig, Shephard French, James Billings, Thomas Dallas, William Simpson, Michael H. Foley, William Stephenson.

EASTERN DISTRICT.

Joseph Anderson, Gay C. Wood, Phillip Vankoughnet, George S. Jarvis, George Anderson, James Pringle, Robert Cline, William Cline, George M. Crysler, William Smart, jun., Jacob F. Pringle, John S. Macdonell, Alexander McMartin, John Crysler, John P. Crysler, John Buckus, Alexander Fraser, Donald McNicol, Alex. Mackenzie, John McLennan, Angus McPherson, John McDonell, Archibald McLean, Alex. Wylie, Peter Shaver, George McDonell, Peter Freel, Angus McGillivray, William K. McKenzie, Alexander McDonell, Rolland McDonald, John Walker, Alexander McDonell, James D. Pringle, Peter John McDonell, Isaac Newton Rose, James Holden, Donald McDonell, D. W. Macauley.

PRINCE EDWARD DISTRICT.

John McCuaig, D. L. Fairfield, Phillip Low, John A. McPherson, Samuel Mirrill, David Barker, Paul E. Washburn, Cecil Mortimer, Thomas Demorset, John P. Roblin, Arch. McFaul, Hon. Robert C. Wilkins, John Low, Samuel Solmes, Robert J. Everitt, George Eyre Henderson, P. McPherson, Thomas Nash, —— Smart.

MIDLAND DISTRICT.

Thomas Kirkpatrick, John K. Forsyth, Henry Smith, jun., Daniel Farley, John A. McDonald, Simon H. Macaulay, Alexander Pringle, James Nickalls, Christopher Armstrong, William B. Smith, Thomas Green, Charles Oliver, Thomas M. Robinson, George A. Cumming, A. H. Dobbs, Charles Stuart, F. C. Muttleburg, Henry Smith, Archibald McDonell, Benjamin Seymour, Henry Lasher, William J. Mackay, William Fairfield, John Feynson, Joseph Allen, Thomas Ramsey, Joshua B. Lockwood, John A. McPherson, Robert Talbot, R. E. Burns, Alexander Campbell, Stafford, F. Kirkpatrick, James Alexander Henderson, John F. Taylor, John Breakenridge, John Stewart Smith, James I. Barrowes, Douglas Prentiss, Francis M. Hill, John C. Davy, George Eyre Hendrson.

VICTORIA DISTRICT.

Benjamin Dougal, Edmund Murney, John Low, Lewis Walbridge, John Ross, Charles C. Benson, Wellington Murney, Thomas Parker, Robert C. A. McLean, Adam H. Meyers, William H. Ponton, John Brooks Crowe, William Smart, Robert John Everitt, John C. Davy Charles L. Coleman, W. Bowen, T. Dalton, J. Breakenridge, G. E. Henderson.

NIAGARA DISTRICT.

Thomas McCormick, Robert Dickson, William H. Merritt, Jacob Keefer, Charles Richardson, Edward C. Campbell, Johnson Clench, C. B. Secord, Warren Claus, William D. Miller, Walter Dickson, George Rykert, W. B. Winterbottom, James Cummings, Alexander Douglass, Alpheus St. John, William McKenzie, Richard A. Clarke, Andrew H. Powell, David Thompson, Thomas H. Taylor, James Hector McKenzie, Francis Webster, John Walker, Marcus Blair, Archibald Gilkison, John T. Taylor, Henry Mittleberger, Thomas Brown, David Thorburn, George W. J. Brock, John B. Lewis, jun., John Stark, Richard Miller, Alexander Duff, Henry Eccles, A. C. Hamilton, George Boomer, Daniel McDougal, Bernard Foley, H. B. Hopkins, Bernard F. Ball, John Armour, Charles J. Robinson, Bernard Clench, Duncan McFarland, John M. Lawder, Henry Graham, Thomas Canby, James Henry Cummings, Joseph Woodruff, Henry Smith, Thomas F. Sampson, Benjamin R. Ottley, R. E. Burns, John Powell, David Thompson, Alexander Scobie, Ronald McKinnon, Honorable James Kerby, Peter Ball Nelles, Robert Henry, John Salmon Minor, Elias Smith Adams.

WELLINGTON DISTRICT.

William D. Powell, Henry McCrum, John Miller, Adam J. Fergusson, William Hewat, Thomas Saunders, Robert Alling, James Webster, Robert B. Miller, Rutherford Muttlebury, D. Bernhard, Warmstead Kirkpatrick.

Board of Education, Canada West.

Chairman—Rt. Rev. Michael, Roman Catholic Bishop of Toronto.
Superintendent of Schools—The Rev. Egerton Ryerson.
The Rev. H. J. Grasett, the Hon. S. B. Harrison, Joseph C. Morrison, Hugh Scobie, and J. S. Howard, Esquire.
Recording Clerk—J. George Hodgins.

The Board of Education hold their meetings, for the present, at the Education Office, Bay-street, Toronto, on Tuesday mornings, at ten o'clock.

Communications for the Board, to be addressed to the Superintendent of Schools for Upper Canada, Toronto.

CIRCUIT COURTS.

District.	District Town.	Spring Circuit, 1847. Days of Opening.	Fall Circuit, 1847. Days of Opening.
Bathurst	Perth	Tuesday, May 11	Thursday, Oct. 28.
Brock	Woodstock,	Monday, May 10	
Colborne	Peterboro'		Monday, Oct. 25.
Dalhousie	Bytown	Wednesday, May 5	Friday, Oct. 22.
Eastern	Cornwall	Wednesday, April 28,	Monday, Oct. 11.
Gore	Hamilton	Wednesday, April 28,	Tuesday, Sept. 29.
Home	Toronto	Tuesday, May 11	Thursday, Oct. 7.
Huron	Goderich	Friday, May 21	
Johnstown	Brockville	Tuesday, April 22	Monday, Oct. 4.
London	London	Thursday, May 13	Tuesday, Sept. 21.
Midland	Kingston	Tuesday, April 13	Friday, Sept. 24.
Newcastle	Cobourg	Tuesday, June 1	Monday, Oct. 18.
Niagara	Niagara	Tuesday, April 13	Monday, Sept. 13.
Prince Edward,	Picton		Wednesday, Oct. 6.
Simcoe	Barrie		Thursday, Oct. 21.
Talbot	Simcoe	Friday, May 14	
Victoria	Bellville	Wednesday, May 26,	Monday, Oct. 11.
Wellington	Guelph	Wednesday, May 26,	
Western	Sandwich	Tuesday, May 4	Monday, Sept. 13.
Ottawa	L'Original		Monday, Oct. 18.

University of King's College, Toronto.

Chancellor—His Excellency the Right Hon. the Earl of Elgin and Kincardine, Governor General of British North America, &c.

Visitors—The Hon. the Judges of the Queen's Bench.

President—The Hon. and Right Rev. John Strachan, D.D., Lord Bishop of Toronto.

Council—The Hon. the Speaker of the Legislative Council; the Hon. the Speaker of the House of Assembly; the Attorney General, Canada West; the Solicitor General; Rev. John McCaul, LL.D., Vice President, and Professor of Classical Literature, &c.; Rev. James Beaven, D.D., Professor of Divinity, &c.; Henry Holmes Croft, Esq., Professor of Chemistry, &c.; Wm. C. Gwynne, B.M., Professor of Anatomy, &c.; John King, M.D., Professor of Medicine; the Principal of Upper Canada College.

Registrar and Bursar—Henry Boys, M.D.

PROFESSORS.

1843. Rev. John McCaul, LL.D., Vice President, and Professor of Classical Literature, Belles Lettres, Rhetoric and Logic.

1843. Rev. James Beaven, D.D., Dean, Professor of Divinity, Metaphysics and Moral Philosophy.

1843. Henry Holmes, Croft, Esq., Proctor, Professor of Chemistry and Experimental Philosophy.

1843. W. C. Gwynne, M.B., Professor of Anatomy and Physiology.

1843. John King, M.D., Professor of the Theory and Practice of Medicine.

1843. William Hume Blake, B.A., Professor of Law and Jurisprudence.

1843. Wiliam Beaumont, F.R.C.S.E., Professor of the Principles and Practice of Surgery.

1843. George Herrick, M.D., Professor of Midwifery and Diseases of Women and Children.

1843. W. B. Nicol, Esq., Professor of Materia Medica and Pharmacy.

1843. Henry Sullivan, M.R.C.S.E., Professor of Practical Anatomy and Curator of Museum.

1844. Rev. Robert Murray, Professor of Mathematics and Natural Philosophy.

1845. Lucius O'Brien, M.D., Professor of Medical Jurisprudence.

Hebrew Tutor—J. M. Hirschfelder, Esq.

The Academical Terms are three — Michaelmas, Hilary and Easter; and the Terminal Dues, payable by students in the Faculty of Arts, are £4 currency, including all charges for tuition.

Those who are desirous of attending particular courses of lectures, although not members of the University, may be admitted as occasional students, but such attendance will not be regarded as a qualification for a degree.

In October, 1846, the College Council established seventy-two Scholarships; three for each of the districts into which Upper Canada is divided, six for Upper Canada College, and six for the University. They are tenable for three years; and the advantages to be enjoyed during that period are, by the District and U. C. College scholars, exemption from all dues and fees; and by the University scholars, in addition to the above, the privilege of rooms and commons without charge. The first Examination is to take place in October, 1847.

———

Upper Canada College Toronto.

(Incorporated with the University of King's College.)

Principal—F. W. Barron, Esq., M.A.

Masters—Rev. Henry Scadding, M.A., 1st Classical Master.
Rev. G. Maynard, M.A., Mathematical Master.

Rev. W. H. Ripley, B.A., 2nd Classical Master.
Mr. W. Stennett, B.A., 3rd Classical Master.
Mr. De la Haye, French Master.
Mr. Barrett, 1st English Master.
Mr. John Gouinlock, 2nd English Master.
Mr. Howard, Geometrical Drawing Master.

COURSE OF EDUCATION.

Greek, Latin, French; Mathematics (Geometry, Algebra, Trigonometry, Logarithms, Conic Sections, &c.), Elements of Natural Philosophy; History, Geography, Use of the Globes, Arithmetic, Mensuration, Book-keeping, Geometrical Drawing, Surveying and Perspective, in addition to the ordinary branches of English; with composition in English and French, and in Greek and Latin prose and verse.

COLLEGE QUARTERS.

First Quarter, from end of Summer Vacation to Chistmas Vacation (about 20th December).
Second Quarter, from end of Christmas Vacation to 20th March.
Third Quarter, from 20th March to 3rd June.
Fourth Quarter, from 3rd June to Midsummer Vacation, about 6th of August.

At whatever period of any of the above quarters a pupil may be entered or withdrawn, his dues for tuition are payable for the whole of that quarter.

All pupils, whose names are on the roll, are charged with the dues, unless notice has been given of their removal from the institution.

Twelve Exhibitions were founded by the Council of King's College, 1841. They are tenable for three years. Accordingly, the regular number of vacancies each year is four; to two of which is attached exemption from College dues for tuition—to one, in addition to the above, the annual stipend of £10—and to one, exemption from College dues for both Board and Tuition, with the liberty to commute the privilege of boarding for an annual stipend of £20.

———

Queen's College and University, Kingston.

PROFESSORS.

Principal and Primarius Professor of Theology — Rev. John Machar.

Professor of Systematic Theology—Rev. James George.

Professor of Biblical Theology and Church History—Rev. Hugh Urquhart.

*Professor of Mathematics, Logic, and Natural Philosophy—*Rev. James Williamson.

*Professor of Classical Literature and Moral Philosophy —*Rev. George Romanes.

The Session of College for students in the Faculty of Arts, lasts for eight months in the year, viz., from the 1st October to 1st June. The Divinity Classes are taught for six months, viz., from 1st November to 1st May.

*Board of Trustees—*Rev. Hugh Urquhart, A.M. ; Rev. John Barclay, A.M.; Rev. John Machar, A.M.; Rev. John Cruickshank, A.M.; Rev. Alex. Mathieson, D.D.; Rev. Principal Liddell, D.D.; Hon. John McDonald; Edward W. Thomson; John Cameron; George Malloch; F. A. Harper, *Treasurer*; Hon. J. Hamilton, *Chairman*; Rev. G. Romanes, A.M.; Rev. James George; Rev. P. C. Campbell, A.M.; Rev. John Cook, D.D.; Rev. Robert McGill; Hon. Archibald McLean; Hon. Peter McGill; Dr. William Craigie ; John Boston; John Mowat; John Thompson; Hon. James Crooks; Hon. William Morris.

University of Victoria College, Cobourg.

*Trustees—*Rev. John Ryerson; Rev. Anson Green; Rev. Richard Jones; Rev. Egerton Ryerson, D.D.; Rev. C. R. Allison; Rev. C. Vandusen ; John P. Roblin, M.P.P. ; Charles Biggar, Esq.; Dr. John Beatty.

*Visitors—*Rev. Henry Wilkinson; Rev. Hamilton Biggar; Rev. Wm. McCullough; Rev. John Carrol; Rev. John Beatty.

*College Senate—*Hon. the President of the Executive Council; Hon. the Speaker of the Legislative Council; Hon. the Speaker of the Legislative Assembly; Hon. the Attorney General, West; Hon. the Solicitor General, West ; Rev. Egerton Ryerson, D.D.; Rev. Alexander MacNab, A.M.; Rev. Jesse Hurlburt, A.M.; William Kingston, Esq., A.M.; John Beatty, Esq., M.D.; Rev. John Ryerson; Rev. Anson Green; Rev. Richard Jones; Rev. Henry Wilkinson; Rev. C. R. Allison; Rev. Hamilton Biggar; Rev. John Carrol; Rev. John Beatty; Rev. C. Vandusen; Rev. W. McCullough; John P. Roblin, Esq., M.P.P.; Charles Biggar, Esq.

FACULTY.

*Principal and Professor of Theology and Moral Science—*Rev. Egerton Ryerson, D.D.

*Vice Principal and Professor of Rhetoric and Belles Lettres—*Rev. Alexander Macnab, M.A.

Professor of Classical Literature—Rev. Jesse Hurlburt, M.A.
Professor of Mathematics—William Kingston, M.A.
Professor of Natural Science—John Beatty, M.D.
Classical Tutor—William Ormiston.
English Teacher—Charles M. D. Cameron.

Knox's College, in connection with Presbyterian Church of Canada, Toronto.

Principal and Primarius Professor of Divinity.—Rev. Robert Burns D. D.
Professor of Systematic Theology.————————
Professor of Classical Literature.—Rev. Alexander Gale, A. M.
Professor of Intellectual and Moral Philosophy.—Rev. H. Esson, A. M.
Professor of Hebrew and Biblical Criticism—Rev. William Rintoul, A. M. *(pro. temp.)*

Toronto Academy, in connection with Presbyterian Church of Canada.

Head Master—Rev. Alexander Gale, A. M.
Teachers—Mr. Thomas Wightman; Mr. Thomas Henning.

Burlington Ladies' Academy, Hamilton.

Visiting and Examining Committee. — Rev. Egerton Ryerson, D.D., Rev. William Case, Rev. John Ryerson, Dr. Kellogg, Samuel B. Freeman, Esq., Rev. Alexander Gale, A. M., Rev. John Roaf, Rev. John Douse, Rev. N. F. English, P. Thornton, Esquire.

OFFICERS OF INSTRUCTION AND GOVERNMENT.

Principal—Rev. D. C. Van Norman, A. M. Preceptress, and Teacher of Drawing, Painting, Perspective, and Vocal Music —Mrs. D. C. Van Norman. First Teacher of English Branches—Miss Jane Van Norman. Teacher of Piano Forte and Guitar—Miss Anne McIntosh. Second Teacher of English Branches, and Assistant Teacher of Drawing and Music—Miss Jane Ann Wright. Teacher of French and German Languages—Mademoiselle Henrietta C. Rothpletz. Teacher of Writing, Needle Work, and Assistant Teacher of Piano Forte—Miss Maria Zwick. Teacher of the Harp—Mrs. Strange. Teacher of Juvenile Department—Miss Olive Wheeler.

List of the Clergy of the United Church of England and Ireland in the Diocese of Toronto.

Lord Bishop of Toronto—The Honourable and Right Reverend John Strachan, D.D., LL.D.

Archdeacon of York—The same.

Archdeacon of Kingston—Venerable George O'Kill Stuart, LL.D.

Examining and Domestic Chaplain and Secretary to the Lord Bishop—The Rev. H. J. Grasett, M.A.

HOME DISTRICT.

City of Toronto.
- Hon. and Right Rev. John Strachan, D.D., LL.D., Rector.
- Rev. H. J. Grasett, M.A., Assistant Minister and Officiating Chaplain to the Forces.
- Rev. Henry Scadding, M.A., Assistant in the Parish, and Chaplain to the Lord Bishop.
- Rev. W. Honywood Ripley, B.A., Minister of Trinity Church.
- Rev. J. Beaven, D.D.
- Rev. John McCaul, LL.D.
- Rev. J. G. D. McKenzie.
- Rev. George Maynard.
- Rev. Charles Ruttan.

CONGREGATIONS.	MINISTERS.
Etobicoke	Thomas Phillips, D.D., Rector.
Toronto Township	James Magrath, M.A. Rector.
York Mills	Alexander Sanson.
Streetsville	Robert J. McGeorge.
Thornhill	Dominick E. Blake, A.B., Rector.
Markham and Vaughan	V. P. Mayerhoffer, M.A., Rector.
Newmarket	George Charles Street.
Georgina	John Gibson.
Brock	R. Garrett.
Whitby	John Pentland, B.A.
Scarboro'	W. Stewart Darling.
Lloydtown	Henry Bath Osler.
Chinguacousy	G. Steven J. Hill.

SIMCOE DISTRICT.

Barrie and Shanty Bay	S. B. Ardagh, A.M.
Tecumseth and W. Gwillimbury	Featherston Lake Osler, M.A.
Orillia	John McIntyre.
Penetanguishene	George Hallen, B.A.
Missionary in the District	G. Bourn.

GORE DISTRICT.

CONGREGATIONS.	MINISTERS.
Hamilton	J. Gamble Geddes, Rector
Saltfleet and Binbrook	J. Lynne Alexander.
Ancaster and Dundas	William McMurray, Rector.
Brantford	J. Campbell Usher.
Wellington Square	Thomas Greene, A.B.
Galt	Michael Boomer, A.B.
Paris	William Morse.
Oakville	Alexander Pyne, A.B.
Trafalgar	George Graham.
Missionaries to the Six Nation Indians on the Grand River	Abraham Nelles and Adam Elliot.

WELLINGTON DISTRICT.

Guelph	Arthur Palmer, A.B., Rector.
Travelling Missionary	—— Frazer.

NIAGARA DISTRICT.

Niagara	Thomas Creen, Rector, Officiating Chaplain to the Forces.
Grimsby	George R. F. Grout, Rector.
Chippewa, Stamford, Queenston and Drummondville	W. Leeming, Rector.
Thorold	Thomas Brock Fuller, Rector.
Fort Erie	John Anderson, Rector.
St. Catharines	A. F. Atkinson, Rector, R. Shanklin
Louth	G. Mortimer Armstrong.
Mouth of the Grand River and Dunnville	Adam Townley.
Settlements on the Grand River	B. Cudmore Hill, M.A.
Binbrook	J. L. Alexander.

TALBOT DISTRICT.

Woodhouse	Francis Evans, Rector.
Simcoe	George Salmon.

LONDON DISTRICT.

London	B. Cronyn, M.A., Rector, Officiating Chaplain to the Forces.
London Township	C. Crosbie Brough, A.B. Rector.
St. Thomas	Mark Burnham, B.A., Rector.
Adelaide	Arthur Mortimer, Rector.
Carradoc	Richard Flood, M.A., Rector.
Port Burwell	T. Bolton Read.
Travelling Missionary	James Stewart.

BROCK DISTRICT.

CONGREGATIONS.	MINISTERS.
Burford	George Petrie.
Woodstock	William Bettridge, B.D., Rector
Oxford	Vacant.
Zorra	F. Fauquier.

HURON DISTRICT.

Goderich	R. Francis Cambell, M.A.
Stratford	John Hickie.
McGillivray	H. C. Cooper.
Colborne	John Wilson.

WESTERN DISTRICT.

Sandwich	William Ritchie, Rector.
Amherstburgh	Fred. Mack, Rector, Officiating Chaplain to the Forces.
Colchester	F. Gore Elliott.
Chatham	William Henry Hobson.
Warwick	James Mockridge.
Moore	Alexander Pyne, A.B.
Walpole Island	Andrew Jamieson.
Dawn, &c	John Gunne.
Raleigh, &c	Francis Wm. Sandys.

NEWCASLE DISTRICT.

Cobourg	A. N. Bethune, D. D., Rector, Chaplain to the Lord Bishop, and Diocesan Prof. of Theology. R. H. Brent.
Port Hope	Jonathan Shortt, Rector.
Cavan	Samuel Armour, Rector.
Clarke and Darlington	T. Smith Kennedy, Rector.
Grafton and Colborne	John Wilson.
Travelling Missionary	Robert Harding.
Murray	P. G. Bartlett.

COLBORNE DISTRICT.

Peterboro'	Robt. J. C. Taylor, M.A., Rector.
Emily	R. A. Harding
Fenelon Falls	Thomas Fidler.

VICTORIA DISTRICT.

Belleville	Rev. John Grier, M.A.

PRINCE EDWARD DISTRICT.

Picton	William Macaulay, Rector.
Carrying Place	W. Greig.

MIDLAND DISTRICT.

CONGREGATIONS.   MINISTERS.

Kingston {
Venerable George O'Kill Stuart, LL.D., Rector.
W. Macaulay Herchmer, M.A., Assistant Minister and Chaplain to the Lord Bishop.
R. Vashon Rogers, Chaplain to the Prov. Penitentiary.
J. H. M. Bartlett, M.A., Off'g Chaplain to the Forces.

Wolf Island ....J. Antisell Allen.
Bath.......... ....W. F. Stuart Harper, Rector.
Adolphuston ....Job Deacon, Rector.
Mohawk and Napanee ....Saltern Givins.
Amherst Island ....John Rothwell, A.B.
Camden, Loughborough, and } Paul Shirley.
   Portland .... {

JOHNSTOWN DISTRICT.

Brockville ....Edward Denroche, M.A.
Lamb's Pond...................William H. Gunning, A.B.
Prescott ....Robert Blakey, Rector.
Kemptville ....Harvey McAlpin.
Merrickville ....Eben Morris.

BATHURST DISTRICT.

Perth ....Michael Harris, M.A., Rector.
Carleton Place ....J. A. Mulock.
Franktown..... ....James William Padfield, Rector.
Smith's Falls ....F. Tremayne.
Pakenham and Fitzroy ....Hannibal Mulkins.

DALHOUSIE DISTRICT.

Bytown ....S. Spratt Strong.
Richmond ....John Flood.
March ....Matthew Kerr.
Fitzroy ....Hannibal Mulkins.

EASTERN DISTRICT.

Cornwall.....................Henry Patten, Rector.
Williamsburgh ....E. Jukes Boswell, Rector.
Osnabruck....................Romaine Rolph.

Manitoulin Island.............Fred. Augustus O'Meara, A.B.

Travelling Missionary in the Diocese—Richard Garrett

Officers of the Church Society of the Diocese of Toronto.

Patrons—His Excellency the Governor General; the Venerable Society for Promoting Christian Knowledge; the Venerable Society for the Propagation of the Gospel in Foreign Parts.

President—The Hon. and Right Rev. the Lord Bishop of the Diocese.

Vice-Presidents—The Honourables Mr. Chief Justice Robinson, R. B. Sullivan, Mr. Vice-Chancellor Jameson, L. P. Sherwood, Mr. Justice Macaulay, Mr. Justice Jones, Mr. Justice Hagerman, P. B. De Blaquiere, Robert Baldwin, M.P.P., William H. Draper, M.P.P., John Macaulay, James Gordon; the Rev. John McCaul, LL.D.; the Rev. James Beaven, D.D.; Henry John Boulton, Esquire; John B. Askin, Esquire; Thomas Mercer Jones, Esquire; the Honourables Colonel Wells, Capt. Boswell, Z. Burnham, Thomas A. Stewart, William Dickson, James Kerby, William Allan, George Crookshank, Robert C. Wilkins, Philip Vankoughnet, John S. Macaulay, Henry Sherwood, M.P.P.; Sir Allan N. Macnab, M.P.P.; Guy C. Wood, Esquire; Frederick Widder, Esquire; Mr. Sheriff Jarvis; Mr. Sheriff Ruttan; the Chairmen of the District Associations.

Standing Committee—The Rev. Official Bethune, D.D.; the Revs. H. J. Grasett, M.A., H. Scadding, M.A., Thomas Green, A. F. Atkinson, J. G. Geddes, D. E. Blake, A.B., T. S. Kennedy, Alexander Sanson; Clarke Gamble, Esquire; L. O'Brien, Esquire, M.D.; F. W. Barron, Esquire, M.A.; Alexander Dixon, Esquire; William Atkinson, Esquire; Alex. Burnside, Esquire: Robert Stanton, Esquire; William Proudfoot, Esquire; James G. Chewett, Esquire; John G. Spragge, Esquire.

Land Committee—The Hon. John H. Cameron; James G. Chewett, Esquire; Ogden Creighton, Esquire.

Auditors—William Proudfoot, Esquire; Lewis Moffatt, Esquire.

Treasurer—Thomas H. Birchall, Esquire.

Secretary—The Rev. W. H. Ripley, B.A.

Assistant Secretary—Thomas Champion, Esquire.

List of the Roman Catholic Clergy of Upper Canada.

DIOCESE OF TORONTO.

Bishop of Toronto—The Right Rev. Michael Power, D.D.

Vicar General—Very Rev. William P. McDonald, Hamilton.

Secretary of the Diocese—Rev. John J. Hay.

Under Secretary—Jeremiah D. Ryan.

Assistant—Rev. T. T. Kirwan, Toronto.

CONGREGATIONS.	CLERGYMEN.
Sandwich	P. Point, and J. A. Menet.
Maidstone	James Jaffray.
Walpole Island	M. Duranquet.
Manitoulin Island	J. J. Chone, J. Hannipaux.
St. Mary's Falls	J. Pedelupé.
Amherstburgh	P. J. Beaupré.
East Tilbury	J. B. Morin.
St. Thomas and London	M. R. Mills.
Brantford	James Quinlan.
Goderich	Peter Schneider.
Wilmot	Simon Sanderl.
Indiana	William McIntosh.

Vicar General—Very Rev. William P. McDonald, Hamilton.

Assistant—Rev. John O'Reily, Wellington Square, &c.

Dundas	Patrick O'Dwyer.
St. Catherines	W. P. M'Donagh.
Niagara	Edward Gordon.
Gore of Toronto	E. O'Reiley.
Newmarket	J. B. Proulx.
Penetanguishene	A. Charest.

DIOCESE OF KINGSTON.

Bishop of Kingston—Right Rev. Remigius Gaulin, D.D.

Coadjutor and Administrator of the Diocese—Right Rev. Patrick Phelan, D.D., Bishop of Carlow.

Vicar General—Very Rev. Augus McDonell, Kingston.

Kingston	{ Patrick Dolland. J. Chisholn, D.D. Alex. McDonald.
Bytown	{ P. A. Telmen. P. Molloy.
Peterborough	James Butler.
Lyndsay	Patrick McEvoy.
Belleville	Michael Brennan.
Tyendinaga	Charles Burke.
Picton	Murth Lawler.
Loborough	Michael McDonnell,
Brockville	Oliver Kelly.
Prescott	Edmund Roach.

DIOCESE OF KINGSTON (*continued*).

CONGREGATIONS.	CLERGYMEN.
Fitzroy	J. McNulty.
St. Andrew's, Stormont	George A. Hay.
Glengarry	J. McDonald, V. G.
Alexandria	Denis Begley.
Mariatown	Bernard Coyle.
Cornwall	John Cannon.
Kitley	Philipp O'Reiley.
Perth	J. H. McDonagh.
Richmond	P. O'Connell.
Kemptville	Daniel Farrell.
L'Orignal	John Farrell.
Eldon	Hugh Fitzpatrick.
Cobourg	J. Timlin.

Clergy of the Presbyterian Church of Canada, in connection with the Church of Scotland.

PRESBYTERY OF TORONTO. *Clerk.*—REV. ANDREW BELL, *Toronto Township. Meets at Toronto on the third Tuesday of February, May, August, and November.*

CONGREGATIONS.	MINISTERS.
Toronto Township	Andrew Bell.
Esquesing	Peter Ferguson.
Scarborough	James George.
Chinguacousy	Thomas Johnson.
King	John Tawse, A. M.
Mono	Alexander Lewis.
Pickering and Whitby	James Lambie, A. M.
Eldon	John McMurchy.
Toronto City, St. Andrew's	John Barclay, A. M.
West Gwillimbury and Innisfil	Alexander Ross.
Clarke and Hope	Samuel Porter.
Vaughan	Rev. P. McNaughton.

PRESBYTERY OF MONTREAL. *Clerk.*—REV. WALTER ROACH, *Beauharnois. Meets at Montreal on the first Wednesday of February, May, August, and November.*

Montreal, St. Andrews	Alexander Mathieson, D. D.
Dundee	Duncan Moody.
Chatham	William Mair.
Beauharnois	Walter Roach.
Ormestown	James Anderson.
Quebec, St. Andrew's	John Cook, D. D.

PRESBYTERY OF MONTREAL (*continued*).

CONGREGATIONS.	MINISTERS.
Georgetown	James C. Muir.
Lachine	William Simpson.
St. Eustache	David Shanks.
Hemmingsford	John Marlin.
Montreal, French Church	Emile Lapelletrie.
Laprairie	John Davidson.
Three Rivers	James Thom.
Huntingdon	Alexander Wallace.
Montreal, St. Paul's	Robert McGill.

PRESBYTERY OF GLENGARY. *Clerk.*—REV. T. McPHERSON, A.M., *Lancaster. Meets on the third Wednesday of January, April, July, and October.*

Williamstown	John McKenzie, A. M.
Cornwall	Hugh Urquhart, A. M.
Martintown	John Maclaurin.
Osnabruck	Isaac Purkis.
Williamsburgh	John Dickey.
Lancaster	Thomas McPherson, A. M.
L'Original	Colin Grigor.

PRESBYTERY OF HAMILTON. *Clerk.*—REV. JOHN CRUICKSHANK, A. M., *Niagara. Meets at Hamilton on the second Wednesday in January, May, and October.*

Nelson	William King.
Mount Pleasant	John Irving.
Clinton	George McClatchey.
Niagara	John Cruickshank, A. M.
Hamilton	Alexander McKid.

PRESBYTERY OF BATHURST. *Clerk.*—REV. WILLIAM BAIN, *Perth. Meets at Perth on the second Wednesday of January, May, and September.*

Beckwith	John Smith.
Smith's Falls	George Romanes, A. M.
Perth	William Bell.
South Gower	Joseph Anderson, A. M.
Packenham	Alexander Mann, A. M.
Richmond	David Evans.
Lanark	Thomas Fraser.
Buckingham and Cumberland	George Bell.
Perth, St. Andrews	William Bain.
Ramsay	John McMorine.
Dalhousie	John Robb.

PRESBYTERY OF KINGSTON. *Clerk.*—REV. JAMES WILLIAMSON, A. M., *Kingston. Meets at Kingston on the first Wednesday of every month.*

CONGREGATIONS.	MINISTERS.
Kingston, St. Andrew's	John Machar, A. M.
Seymour	Robert Neill.
Queen's College, Kingston	James Williamson, A. M.

Lay Association in support of the Presbyterian Church of Canada, in connection with the Church of Scotland, Montreal.

ELECTED 1st NOVEMBER, 1845.

President—Hon. Peter McGill.
Vice Presidents—T. Wilson, J. Fisher, R. Armour, A. Shaw.
Treasurer—Andrew H. Armour.
Recording Secretary—William Edmonstone.
Corresponding Secretary—Hew Ramsay.
Managers—D. Stewart, John Armour, James Young, Neil McIntosh, James Scott, William Dow, John Frothingham, John Greenshields, John Smith, J. G. Mackenzie, A. Cowan, John Birss, H. E. Montgomerie.
Chaplains—Rev. Dr. Mathieson, Rev. R. McGill.

Presbyterian Church of Canada.

PRESBYTERY OF HAMILTON.

CONGREGATIONS.	MINISTERS.
Hamilton	
Dundas and Ancaster	Mark Y. Stark.
Zorra	Donald McKenzie.
Galt	John Bayne.
Thorold	Angus McIntosh.
Stratford	David Allan.
Puslinch	William Meldrum.
Grimsby	Daniel Eastman.
Port Sarnia	William McAlister.
Saltfleet and Binbrook	George Cheyne.
Ayr	Robert Lindsay.
Fergus	George Smellie.
Amherstburgh	Robert Peden.
Tuckersmith	William Graham.
St. Thomas	John McKinnon.
Caledonia	Andrew Ferrier, D.D.

Mark Y. Stark, *Presbytery Clerk.*

PRESBYTERY OF TORONTO.

CONGREGATIONS.	MINISTERS.
Toronto	Rev. Robert Burns, D.D.
Streetsville	William Rintoul.
Norval and Union	Peter Gray.

OFFICIATING WITHIN THE BOUNDS,
Henry Esson, James Harris, Donald McMillan.

William Rintoul, *Presbytery Clerk.*

PRESBYTERY OF COBOURG.

Cavan South	James Douglas.
Peterborough and Cavan	John M. Rogers.
Cobourg	Thomas Alexander.
Grafton and Colborne	William Reid.
Darlington	Alexander Steele.

William Reid, *Presbytery Clerk.*

PRESBYTERY OF KINGSTON.

Picton	William Hamilton.
Demorestville	James Rogers.
Camden	Thomas Wightman.
Kingston, (Bagot-st.)	Robert A. Reid.
Gananoque	Henry Gordon.

OFFICIATING WITHIN THE BOUNDS,
Alexander McLean.

PRESBYTERY OF BROCKVILLE.

Brockville	William Smart.
Prescott	Robert Boyd.
Edwardsburgh	James Geggie.
Osgoode and Gloucester	William Lochhead.
Gower (South)	William McDowell.
Bellamyville	Alexander Luke.

PRESBYTERY OF PERTH.

Bytown	Thomas Wardrope.
Ramsay	William Johnston.
Perth	Andrew Melville.

PRESBYTERY OF MONTREAL.

Quebec	John Clugston.
Indian Lands	Daniel Clarke.
Saint Therese	David Black.
La Chute	Thomas Henry.
Port Neuf	S. C. Frazer.
Montreal (St. Gabriel-st.)	William Leishman.

David Black, *Presbytery Clerk.*

Clergy of the British Wesleyan Conference in Canada West

CONGREGATIONS.	CLERGYMEN.
Amberstburgh	Edward Lallows,
Barrie	John Ross,
Belleville	Henry Lanton,
Brantford and Grand River	Thomas Fawcett,
Brock	William Gundy,
Bytown	John C. Davidson,
Cavan and Peterborough	James Booth and John Bredin,
Chinguacousy	William Steer,
Goderich	Henry Byers,
Guelph	Samuel Fear,
Hamilton	John Douse,
Kingston	Edmund Botterell,
London and Blanchard	Ephraim Evans, Wm. Andrews,
Loughborough	John Slater,
Stratford	John Gundy,
Toronto and Whitchurch	W. M. Harvard, R. Cooney, John Hunt,
Warwick and Adelaide	Charles Turner,
Whitby and Pickering	David Clappison,
Woodstock	Thos W. Constable.

INDIAN MISSIONS.

Alderville	John Sunday, W. Case.
Grand River	Thomas Fawcett,
Rice Lake	James Booth,
St. Clair, Port Sarnia	William Scott,
Wyandotte	E. Sallows.

Chairman—W. M. Harvard.

Secretary—Ephraim Evans.

Financial Secretary—John Douse.

Wesleyan Methodist Church in Canada.

President of the Conference.—Thomas Bevitt.

Secretary.—Hamilton Biggar.

CHAIRMEN OF DISTRICTS.

London.—William Ryerson.
Hamilton.—John Ryerson.
Toronto.—Henry Wilkinson.

Cobourg.—Richard Jones.
Kingston.—Thomas Bevitt.
Bytown.—James Musgrove.

Book Steward.—Anson Green.   *Editor.*—George R. Sanderson.

CIRCUITS.	MINISTERS AND PREACHERS.
London (Station)	Charles Lavell.
London	Cornelius Flumerfelt, William Dignam.
Woodstock	Matthias Holtby, James Gray.
Chatham	William Willoughby, Nathan Axtell.
St. Thomas	Samuel C. Philp, Alexander T. Green.
Brantford	Edwy M. Ryerson, Richard Whiting.
Simcoe	Kennedy Creighton, Francis Chapman.
Norwich	Solomon Snyder.
Malahide	Thomas Jeffers.
Hamilton	William Pollard, Thomas Rattray.
Dundas	Wellington Jeffers, Joseph E. Ryerson.
Dumfries	John Law, Joseph Shepley.
Nelson	James Spencer, Peter Ker.
Grimsby	Matthew Whiting, Thomas Demorest.
St. Catharines	Lewis Warner, George Young.
Stamford	Ruben E. Tupper, E. B. Harper.
Georgetown	William Philp.
Chippewa	Luther O'Rice.
Toronto City	John Carroll, Noble F. English.
Yonge Street	Samuel Rose, George Carr.
Humber	Charles W. M. Gilbert, William Glass.
Toronto Circuit	George Poole, James Hutchinson.
Oshawa	William Price.
Bowmanville	Ozias Barber.
Markham	Ezra Adams, D. Bettys.
Newmarket	John Baxter, John W. Cawthorne.
Bradford	William Coleman, Benjamin Jones.
Cobourg	Jonathan Scott.
Hallowell	Asahel Hurlburt.
Napanee	George Goodson, John Sanderson.
Consecon	William McFadden, Abraham Dayman.
Colborne	Robert Darlington, Nelson Brown.
Sidney	Cyrus R. Allison, John C. Osborne.
Port Hope	John Gemley.
Peterboro'	William McCullough, Thomas Cleghorn.
Demorestville	Isaac B. Aylesworth.
Kingston	Edmund Shepherd.
Waterloo	William Haw, Vincent B. Howard.
Bath	John Black, Joseph Hill.
Gananoque	Alvah Adams.
Elizabethtown	Michael Fawcett.
Brockville	Conrad Vandusen.
Prescott	Joseph Messmore.
Augusta	Joseph W. McCollum.

CIRCUITS.	MINISTERS AND PREACHERS.
Smith's Falls	William H. Williams, William H. Poole.
Newboro'	Matthew Connor.
Matilda	John Lever, James Armstrong.
Cornwall	Simon Huntington, George Case.
Bytown	Lachlin Taylor, Jonathan Loverin.
Perth	David B. Madden, Erastus Hurlburt.
Mississippi	James Hughes, Robert Robinson.
Osgoode	John Armstrong.
Richmond	Benjamin Nankevill, David McDowell.
L'Original	Joseph Reynolds, Thomas Hannah.
Hull	Francis Coleman.
Kemptville	James Elliott.

Supernumerary Preachers.—Moses Blackstock, Daniel McMullen, John Beatty, John Culham, Gilbert Miller, Franklin Metcalf.

Superannuated Preachers.—Andrew Prindle, George Ferguson, David Youmans, James Wilson, Thomas Harmon, Ezra Healy, David Wright, Wyat Chamberlain, William Brown.

MISSIONS.	MISSIONARIES.
Tilbury	David Hardie.
Walpole Island	John Williams.
Warwick	Robert Corson, Thomas Williams.
Muncey	Solomon Waldron, Abram Sickles.
Saugeeng	John K. Williston.
Huron	George Kennedy.
Guelph	Thomas Cosford.
Grand River	Rowley Heyland, Stephen Brownell.
York	Sylvester Hurlburt, John Goodfellow.
Snake Island	Preachers of Newmarket Circuit.
Mono & Nottawasaga	William S. Blackstock.
Barrie	William Graham.
Credit	Samuel Belton, Peter Jones.
Rama	Horace Dean.
St. Vincent	David Jennings.
Brock	William Young, — Campbell.
Owen's Sound	John Neelands.
French River	William Herkimer.
Shannonville	George F. Playter.
Norwood	Richard Phelps.
Cartwright	Robert Lochhead.
Marmora	Stephen Miles.
Sheffield	George Beynon.
Schoogog	George B. Butcher.
Amherst Island	Preachers of Bath Circuit.

B

MISSIONS.	MISSIONARIES.
St. Andrews	Michael Baxter, Charles Taggart.
Buckingham	John Tuke.
Gatineau	William Morton.
Clarendon	James Greener.
Pembroke	Henry Shaler, William Pattyson.
Onslow	John Howes.

Missionary Committee—President and Secretary of the Conference, Superintendent of Toronto City, Chairman of Toronto District, Dr. Ryerson, Superintendent of Yonge-street Circuit, James R. Armstrong, James Hodgson, Robert James, jun., George Walker, Peter Lawrence, and E. C. Benns.

Treasurer—Anson Green.

Corresponding Secretary—George R. Sanderson.

Recording Secretary—Mr. S. S. Junkin.

Clergy of Methodist (New Connexion) Church.

CIRCUITS.	MINISTERS AND PREACHERS.
Ancaster and Nelson	J. Caswell.
Barnston Mission	P. V. West.
Bolton and Potton	K. P. Adams, R. Bowen.
Cavan	B. Haigh, R. Read, W. Robertson.
Crosby and Eliza-bethtown	H. Bursell, C. Childs, N. C. Gowan.
Drummond	T. Rump.
Dunham	T. T. Howard, N. Parker, G. W. Stone, F. E. Powers.
Goulborn	J. Rice.
Hamilton	J. Brennan.
Henrysburgh	F. Hunt.
London	A. Armstrong.
Lansdown	J. C. Warren, L. Olmstead.
Malahide & Norwich	J. Shilton, F. Weaver.
Newcastle	H. Wilkinson.
Owen Sound	J. Simpson.
Prince Edward	J. Hales, T. Haynes.
Raleigh and Howard	J. Bell, A. Wade.
Stukely	J. Histon, P. Lawrence.
Stanstead	J. Blake.
St. Thomas	W. Bothwell.
Trafalgar	E. Bailey.
Waterford	J. Wilkinson, J. Jackson.
Welland Canal	E. VanNorman.

Nassagaweya ······E. Williams.
Toronto··········T. Goldsmith.
Caledon ······ ····W. Ramage.
General Superintendent—H. O. Crofts.
Treasurer—J. Hughes, Esq.

_____

United Secession Synod of Canada, in connection with the United Secession Church of Scotland.

LONDON PRESBYTERY.

CONGREGATIONS.	MINISTERS.
London, Westminster ··········	W. Proudfoot, *Presbytery Clerk,*
Proof Line, English Settlement··	James Skinner,
Blenheim ··················	George Murray,
Tuckersmith, Stanley··········	Alexander McKenzie,
Chatham, East Tilbury ········	James McFadyen,
Paris······················	David Caw.

HAMILTON PRESBYTERY.

West Flamborough ··········	Thomas Christie,
St. George, Brantford··········	James Roy, *Presbytery Clerk,*
West Dumfries ··············	Alexander Ritchie,
Eramosa, Nichol, Elora········	William Barrie,
St. Catharines, Thorold, Port Dalhousie················	John Porteous.
Chippawa···················	Charles Fletcher,
Guelph ····················	Robert Torrance.

TORONTO PRESBYTERY.

Port Hope, Perrytown·········	John Cassie,
Whitby ····················	Robert Thornton,
West Gwillimbury, Tecumseth, Essa ···················	William Fraser.
Clarke (4th con, Newtown, Newcastle ················	George Lawrence.
Toronto City················	John Jennings, *Presbytery Clerk,*
Emily, Ops, Manvers··········	James Dick,
Chinguacousy, Albion, Vaughan	David Coutts,
Richmond Hill, Thornhill ······	Walter Scott.

MONTREAL PRESBYTERY.

Montreal ···················	Wm. Taylor,
La Chute···················	Andrew Kennedy,
New Glasgow················	Alex. Lowden, *Presbytery Clerk,*
Smith's Falls ···············	Wm. Aitken,
Madrid ····················	John Morrison.

Missionaries unsettled—James Dalrymple and James McLelland.

Moderator—William Fraser.

Synod Clerk—William Proudfoot.

THEOLOGICAL INSTITUTE, IN LONDON.

Superintendent—Rev. William Proudfoot.

Period of study in Theology for Licentiates, four years. Two Sessions in each year, of five months each.

Clergy of the Congregational Denomination in C. W.

Asphodel—T. Searight.
Belleville—J. Harris.
Brighton—J. Vincent.
Brock—N. McKinnon.
Brockville—T. Machin.
Brantford—T Baker.
Burford—M. Alworth.
Caledon—S. King.
Darlington—J. Clemie, junior.
Esquesing—H. Dewney.
Glanford—S. Finton.
Glengarry—J. McKilliken.
Georgetown { D. Powel. / J. Armour.
Guelph—E. Martin.
Hamilton { J. Wilkins. / J. Osborne.

Innisfil—J. Clemie.
London—E. Ebbs.
L'Original—J. T. Byrne.
Moore—J. Geikie.
Newmarket—J. Durrant.
Oro—A. Raymond.
Port Dover—J. Marr.
Port Sarnia—J. Nall.
Simcoe—W. Clarke.
Southwold—J. Silex.
Stouffville—L. Kriles.
Stratford—A. Geikie.
St. Thomas—W. P. Wastell.
Toronto—J. Roaf. A Lillie.
Vaughan—T. Hodgkin.
Whitby—T. Snell.

Congregational Academy, Toronto.

Tutor····································Rev. Adam Lillie.

Treasurer·······························Rev. John Roaf.

Secretary·······························Robert Beekman, Esq.

Committee—Rev. John Roaf, Rev. Adam Lillie, — Freeland, Esq., A. T. McCord, Esq., W. D. Taylor, Esq., — Tolfree, Esq.

Clergy of the Baptist Church in Canada.

Ancaster—W. L. Bayley.
Aylmer—S. Baker.
Barford—T. Ide.
Barnston—J. Green.
Beamsville—George Silver.

Osgoode—D. McPhail.
Osnabruck—A. McLean.
Paris { N. Bosworth, F. R. S. / H. Fitch.
Perth—J. Cooper.

Beverly { John Miner.
P. Scholfield.

Blenheim { Francis Pickle.
W. C. Beordsall.

Bloomfield—Joseph Home.

Biddulph—D. A. Turner.

Brantford { J. Winterbottom.
J. H. Carryer.

Breadalbane—William Frazer.

Brighton—J. Holman.

Brock—H. Reid.

Brockville—R. Boyd.

Caledon—J. Campbell.

Canborough—William Cook.

Carlton Place—L. Halcroft.

Chatham { J. King.
E. Highworden.

Cobourg—S. Tapscott.

Crosby, South—M. Eathron.

Dundas—J. Clutton.

Drummondville—A. Cleghorn.

Eaton—A. Gillies.

Equesing—J. Oakley.

Georgeville—E. Mitchell.

Gosfield { R. Henington.
N. French.

Haldimand { William Lacy.
D. Wait.

Hamilton { A. Booker.
—— Brown.

Ingersoll—Isaac Elliot.

Kingston—A. Lorimer.

Lanark { R. Dick.
J. Dick.
J. Smith.

Leeds—A. Stevens.

Lobo—Wm. Wilkinson.

London—N. Eastwood.

Louth—S. H. Goss.

Malahide—George Wilson.

Montreal { J. M. Cramp.
F. Bosworth.
J. Girdwood.

Nissouri—S. Vining.

Peterborough { J. Gilmour.
J. Edwards.

Petite Nation—William Dick.

Port Hope—J. Baird.

Port Rowen—W. McDermid.

Potton, South—T. Merriman.

Quebec—D. Marsh.

Queenston—D. Curry.

Raleigh—William Gorrie.

Rainham—J. Van Loon, Junior.

Rawdon—J. Butler.

Reach—W. Hurlbuet.

Sandwich—George Jacobs.

Scotland—William Drummond.

Short Hills—D. Way.

Sidney—William Geary.

Simcoe—T. Bailey.

Smith's Falls—C. Clutz.

South Gower—P. McDonald.

Southwold—T. Mills.

St. Catherines { W. Hewson.
J. Anderson.

St. George—William Smith.

St. Thomas { R. Andrews.
—— Bray.

Stanbridge—F. N. Jersey.

Thurlow—J. Bridges.

Toronto { R. A. Fyfe.
W. Christian.

Townsend—S. McConnell.

Tuscarora—W. H. Landon.

Vittoria—L. J. Olney.

Walpole—T. Stillwell.

Waterford { Wm. Porterfield.
A. Sloght.
G. J. Ryerse.

Whitby—J. Marsh.

Windham { M. W. Hopkins.
P. Steinhoff.

Woodstock—E. Topping.

Yarmouth—C. Stewart.

York Mills—J. Mitchell.

Zorra—J. S. Manning.

St. George's Society, Toronto.

President—G. P. Ridout, Esq.
Vice Presidents — W. B. Jarvis, Esq.; G. D. Wells, Esq.;
W. Wakefield, Esq.
Chaplains—Rev. H. Scadding, M.A.; Rev. C. Winstanley, M.A.
Physician—Edward Hodder, Esq., M.D.
Managing Committee—Messrs. Bilton, J. D. Ridout, J. Moore,
F. Lewis, T. Brunskill, J. G. Beard.
Treasurer—H. Rowsell, Esq.
Secretary—S. Thompson.
Standard Bearers — Messrs. F. W. Coate, T. Armstrong,
A. Wasnidge, A. Laing.

St. Andrew's Society, Toronto.

President—John Cameron, Esq.
Vice Presidents—Thomas G. Ridout, Esq.; John Robertson, Esq.
Managers—Messrs. William Wilson, John Bell, Thomas Paterson.
Chaplains—Rev. John Barclay, A. M.; Rev. John Jennings.
Physicians—Dr. Telfer; Dr. Hamilton.
Standing Committee — Messrs. Duncan McDonell, John Shaw,
William M. Gorrie, Thomas Ewart.
Committee of Accounts — Messrs. Samuel Spreule, James Leask,
Hugh Miller.
Treasurer—Alexander Badenach, Esq.
Secretary—Mr. Angus Morrison.
Assistant Secretary—Mr. Robert Maitland.
Standard Bearers — Messrs. John Kidd, John Berry, William
Jamieson, James George.
Marshal—Stedman B. Campbell, Esq.

St. Patrick's Society, Toronto.

President—J. H. Hagarty, Esq.
Vice Presidents—John Duggan, Esq.; John King, Esq., M.D.;
Charles Stotesbury, Esq.
Treasurer—John Harrington, Esq.
Secretary—Kivas Tully, Esq.
Committee of Management—Messrs. Joseph Bates, J. R. Mountjoy,
Ashfield, John Ritchey, G. L. Allan, T. McConkey, James
Watkins.
Chaplains—The Rev. John McCaul, L.L.D.; Rev. H. J. Grasett.
Physician—George Herrick, Esq., M.D.
Marshal—Mr. John Craig.
Standard Bearers—Messrs. McClenaghan, Givan, J. J. Evans.

Provincial Grand Lodge of Free Masons, of Upper Canada.

Under the authority of the Grand Lodge of England.

Br. Sir A. N. McNab .... *R. W. P. G. Master.*
" T. G. Ridout .... *R. W. D. P. G. Master.*
Br. Thomas Mercer Jones .... *P. S. G. Warden.*
" C. H. Webster .... *P. J. G. Warden.*
" P. V. Meyerhoffer .... *P. G. Chaplain.*
" A. Burnside .... *P. G. Treasurer.*
" R. McClure .... *P. G. Registrar.*
" Francis Richardson .... *P. G. Secretary.*
" W. A. Campbell .... *P. S. G. Deacon.*
" S. C. Richardson .... *P. J. G. Deacon.*
" Kivas Tully .... *P. Grand Superintendent Works.*
" Antrobus Holwell .... *P. Grand Director Ceremonies.*
" James Henderson .... *Assistant ditto*
" Hugh B. Wilson .... *P. Grand Pursuivant.*

Br. the Sr. Deacon of York Lodge, Grand River,
" " Zetland Lodge, Toronto,
" " St. Andrew's Lodge, Toronto, } *P. Grand*
" " St. John's Lodge, Cobourg, } *Stewards.*
" " Western Light Lodge, Lloydtown,
" " St. John's Lodge, Kingston,
" John Morrison .... *P. Grand Tyler.*

The following ten reasons for emigrating to Canada are reprinted from the *Canadian Almanac* for 1864. A piece of utopian propaganda, aimed primarily at English-speaking peoples from the British Isles, it nevertheless contains items of interest, charm and, from our privileged standpoint, unintended humour.

Once arrived in Canada, the newcomer is informed that "the cost of the passage by deck of steamer and second class cars is, from Quebec to Toronto, about $5". In the Upper Province, land sells for 70 cents per acre. If that land runs out, "we have the North West to fall back upon", made up of the "Red River and Saskatchewan Country". In terms of natural resources, Canada is cast as a land "of untold, almost inconceivable wealth".

The health of the population, as borne out by Canada's comparatively low death rate, is ascribed to the climate: "its cloudless skies, its elastic air, and almost entire absence of fogs". Reports of extreme cold, "often greatly exaggerated", are turned on their heads by the beneficial results of snow and ice, which make for smooth passage over rivers and rough woodland roads, "the whole face of the country being literally macadamized by nature for a people as yet unable to macadamize for themselves". Perhaps the fine print to all this praise is condensed into the last item listed as needful to success here: the blessing of God.

TEN REASONS FOR EMIGRATING TO CANADA.

The aim of the man who contemplates changing the land of his birth for another being, generally speaking, the improvement of his condition, the question where the circumstances may be looked for most favourable to the realization of his desire, claims his best thought. Such thought he owes to himself, to his family if he has one, and to those among whom he may decide on taking up his abode; because mistake in his choice may involve him and those he loves in disappointment and distress, and entail weakness on those to whom he should bring strength.

In favour of the selection of Canada as his future home, the attention of the intending emigrant is respectfully invited to the considerations which follow.

1. *Its accessibility.*

Compared with other regions open to him, it may be reached in a very short time (eleven days by steam), at a trifling expense, and with a small amount of inconvenience.

In sailing vessels, the rates of steerage passage vary, according to accommodation, from three pounds to four or five pounds sterling. The charge between Liverpool, Londonderry or Glasgow, and Toronto, by the Montreal Steamship line, is $34, including provisions; between Glasgow and Quebec or Montreal, $29. By the Anchor Line, the charge between Glasgow and Quebec is $25. The Great Eastern charges $30 between Liverpool and New York. Its cabin rates are—1st cabin, $95–$135; 2d cabin, $70; 3d cabin, $50. By the Montreal Line, the cabin passage varies, with accommodation, from $72–$88. The cabin fare between Glasgow and Quebec, by the Ocean Line, is $68; intermediate, $44. By the Anchor Line, $60; intermediate, $30. Children are carried by them all at lower rates, generally half-price.

Once landed at Quebec or Montreal, the emigrant may pass on to Toronto, or Hamilton, or any intermediate locality, by steamboat or railway; and thence by railway to the western extremity of the province. The Northern Railway will take him to any place he pleases on the route between Toronto and Collingwood, Lake Huron, whence he can pass on to Owen Sound and intermediate places by steamer. The cost of the passage by deck of steamer and second class cars is, from Quebec to Toronto, a distance of 500 miles, about $5; with corresponding rates for places intermediate; to Windsor, the western extremity of the province. 631 miles from Quebec, $7 12½; to Barrie, 565 miles, $6 50; to Collingwood, 593 miles, $7. The time between Quebec and Toronto is by railway about 36 hours, by steamboa a day or two longer. Toronto may be reached by railway from Portland, the ocean terminus of the Grand Trunk, in from 25 to 26 hours.

As, moreover, he may return to his old home so much more easily, should he for any reason wish to do so, he is less ir retrievably committed by coming here than by going elsewhere. A visit to it is also at any time much more practicable, other things being equal. His friends may likewise, if so disposed, follow him with much less of difficulty—thus renewing associations of which necessity had compelled the temporary interruption.

2. *The scope afforded by its extent, both for the successful employment of his capabilities and the gratification of his tastes in the choice of a home.*

Leaving out the territory to the northwest, the opening of which may be looked for ere long, Canada occupies a space, stretching in a south-westerly direction from the Island of Anticosti in the Gulf of St. Lawrence, to the south-western extremity of Lake Erie, of about 1,400 miles in length; with a breadth varying from two hundred to four hundred miles. Including water-surface, it is computed to contain an area of 349,821 square miles—242.482 exclusive of water. The number of acres comprised within it is estimated at 160,405,219—128,659.684 of which are reckoned to Canada East; to Canada West, 31,745,533.

"If an area," it is remarked in a pamphlet published in 1860, by authority, "be traced in Europe, corresponding generally to that occupied by Canada, in America, and the meridian of the most southern part of Canada be supposed to lie upon the meridian of Greenwich, in England, the south of France, at the base of the Pyrenees, will represent the south frontier of Canada; the south-eastern boundary of this area will stretch through France, Swit zerland, Bavaria, and Austria, to a point in the south of Poland, and a line drawn northward to Warsaw will delineate the mouth of the Gulf of St. Lawrence. The north western boundary of this area will extend from the south of France, in a northerly direction, towards and beyond Brest; and a line drawn from near Brest to the British Channel, thence through England, Belgium and Germany, to Warsaw again, will establish the position of a European area, corresponding to Canada in America. The inhabited and highly fertile portion of Canada is represented in this area by those regions which lie in the south, centre and south-east of France, and in those parts of Switzerland, Bavaria and Austria, included within its boundary. The other portion, although of vast extent, and not so well fitted for extended agricultural operations, is highly valuable on account of its timber and minerals.

The Province of Canada embraces about 350,000 square miles of territory, independently of its north-western possessions, not yet open for settlement; it is consequently more than one-third larger than France, nearly three times as large as Great Britain and Ireland, and more than three times as large as Prussia. The inhabited or settled portion covers at least 40,000 square miles, and is nearly twice as large as Denmark, three times as large as Swit zerland, a third greater than Scotland, and more than a third the size of Prussia; but such is the rapid progress of settlement through immigration, that in ten years time the settled parts of Canada will be equal in area to Great Britain or Prussia."

According to the Crown Lands Report for 1856, the peninsula of Gaspé alone, which is 175 miles in length, with an extreme breadth of 90 miles, comprises an area, after the deduction of a small portion covered by New Brunswick, of 11,800 superficial miles, equal to that of the European peninsula of Denmark, which it resembles if form. The Tadousac territory, valued as yet chiefly for its timber trade and its fisheries, is there stated to have a coast of six hundred miles in length on the Gulf and River St. Lawrence, with a breadth of 160 miles and an area of probably 65,000 square miles; more than twice that of Scotland. The country drained by the Saguenay includes an area of 27,000 square miles, an extent equal to the Tyrol and Switzerland taken together. The quantity of land in it capable of cultivation is estimated at about 3,000,000 acres. The area drained by the St. Maurice is about 21,000 superficial miles; about one-tenth larger than the main land of Scotland, and containing about as much arable land. "Admirably watered, and intersected by magnificent rivers, with forests of pine alternating with rich tracts of hardwood land, and with that most valuable of all minerals, iron ore, in unlimited quantities, the country wants but the hand of man and the course of a few years to make it equal to the most flourishing parts of Canada." The area of the Ottawa and tracts therewith connected is estimated at 82,000 miles; one-fourth greater than that of the New England States.

In the Great Manitoulin Island, which contains about 3,000,000 acres, upwards of 200,000 acres are expected soon to come into market. On the north sides of Lakes Huron and Superior there remains to be noticed an area of about 48,000 miles; one-half greater than that of the State of Maine.

Regions so vast afford certainly ample room and verge enough, and will do for some time to come. Should they, however, become too strait, we have the North West to fall back upon, one-fifth of which, the Red River and Saskatchewan country, is computed to contain a territory exceeding in extent the empires of France and Austria united.

3. *The physical characteristics of the country, its natural resources, and its healthfulness.*

The variety of its products and abundance of its harvests attest, where proper care is bestowed on its cultivation, the excellence of its soil. And although in the longer settled parts of the country the best lands may be supposed to be occupied, and therefore attainable only at a considerable advance on the ori. inal prices, others quite equal to them are to be found in the newer regions which every year is bringing into the market. According to the Crown Land report for last year, there are now in the hands of the Government (surveyed) for disposal 5,908,557 acres, in Lower Canada; in Upper Canada, 2,839,358½—in all, 8,747.915½—varying in price with situation.

"In Upper Canada, it is 70 cents per acre for cash. or one dollar when paid in instalments—one at the time of purchase, and the remainder in four equal annual payments with interest. In Lower Canada, the highest price is 60 cents, but the larger quantity is disposable at 30 cents per acre. In the Algoma District, Upper Canada, and in those of Gaspé and Saguenay in Lower Canada, the price is only 20 cents. The condition of settlement is exacted in all cases.

Through these newer lands seven great roads have recently been laid out in Upper and five in Lower Canada. The Upper Canada roads are—1. "The Ottawa and Opeongo road," which runs east and west, intended to be 171 miles in length, and to connect the Ottawa river with Lake Huron,—of this, 62 miles are finished, on which 235 settlers are already located. 2. The "Addington Road," which intersects the Opeongo Road,—on this, which is about 61 miles in length, there are 178 settlers. 3. "The Hastings Road," running nearly parallel to the Addington Road, and connecting the county of Hastings with the Ottawa and Opeongo Road, 68 miles in length.—on which there are 306 settlers. 4. "The Bobcaygeon Road," running north from Bobcaygeon, between the counties of Peterborough and Victoria, meant to be continued to Nipissing,—the number of miles completed is 36, the number of settlers 168. 5. "The Frontenac and Madawaska Road," of which the number of miles completed is 33. 6. "The Muskoka Road," which runs from the head of the navigation of Lake Couchiching to the Grand Falls of Muskoka, where it will intersect what is called Peterson's line, which will eventually meet the Ottawa and Opeongo Road, now gradually opening westwardly. By this road, the intending settler can reach the centre of the county in one day from Toronto, whence he will proceed by Northern Railway to Lake Simcoe, and thence by steamer,—21 miles are completed. 7. "The Sault Ste. Marie Road," intended to run from Sault Ste. Marie to Goulais Bay,—four miles of which are completed.

The five in Lower Canada are "The Elgin Road," in the county of L'Islet, 38 miles in length, from St Jean Port Joli to the Provincial Line; "The Montreal and Cap Chat; "The Taché Road, from Buckland. county of Bellechasse, to Kempt Road, Rimouski, about 200 miles; "The Temiscouata Road," from River du Loup to Lake Temiscouata; and "The Kempt Road," from Metis to Restigouche.

Along these roads, free grants, not exceeding 100 acres

in each case, are given by the government for the purpose of facilitating settlement, on the following conditions.

1. That the settler be eighteen years of age.

2. That he take possession of the land allotted to him within one month.

3. That he put into a state of cultivation 12 acres of land in the course of four years.

4. That he build a log house, 20 by 18 feet, and reside on the lot until the foregoing conditions are fulfilled.

"Families may reside on a single lot, and the several members having land allotted to them will be exempt from building and residence on each individual lot. The non-fulfilment of these conditions will cause the immediate loss of the land, which will be sold or given to another. The lands thus opened up, and gratuitously offered by the government for settlement, are chiefly of excellent quality, and well adapted in respect of soil and climate, to all the purposes of husbandry.

"The reports of the resident agents on these roads, for the past year, convey the most favourable accounts of the prosperity of the settlers thereon, and of the large amount of produce they have raised on the newly-cleared lands."

In the Crown Lands Report for 1862, similar accounts are given; though a late statement excepts certain parts of the Opeongo Road, which are said to be so rocky as to be incapable of cultivation.

In its mines, in its forests, and in its fisheries, Canada has stores of untold, of almost inconceivable wealth; which its numerous lakes and rivers supply facilities for conveying to market.

Of metallic minerals, the following are enumerated in a catalogue contained in "Canada at the Universal Exhibition, in 1855," to wit, Magnetic Iron Ore, Specular Iron Ore, Limonite (Bog Ore), Titaniferous Iron, Sulphate of Zinc (Blende), Sulphate of Lead (Galena), Copper, Nikel, Silver, Gold. Non-metallic—Teranium, Chromium, Cobalt, Manganese, Iron Pyrites, Graphite, Dolomite, Carbonate of Magnesia, Sulphate of Baryta, Iron Ochres, Steatite, Lithographic Stone, Agates, Jasper, Labradore Felspar, Aventurine, Hyacinthe, Corumdum, Amethyst, Jet, Quartzose Sandstone, Retinite and Basalt, Gypsum. Shell Marl, Phosphate of Lime, Millstones, Grindstones, Whetstones, and Tripoli. Under the head "Building Materials," are specified. Granites, Sandstone, Calcarous Sandstone, Limestones, Hydraulic Limestones, Roofing Slates, Flagging Stones; Clays suitable for the formation of red and white bricks, tiles and coarse pottery; Moulding Sand, Fuller's Earth; and Marbles, white, black, red, brown, yellow and black, grey and variegated, and green. Of combustibles—Peat, Petroleum and Asphaltum, are named. Some of these are confined to a single locality, others to a few places, but the more useful of them are widely distributed and their quantities very great.

Though our fisheries are as yet in their infancy, they employ from 1,200 to 1,500 boats, with nearly 100 vessels. The annual value of their products is, for Lower Canada, $942,528; for Upper Canada, $380,000; total, $1,322,528.

Exclusive of furs, the products of the forest amounted, in 1860, to $11,012,253.

Our climate, notwithstanding the extremes of cold and heat to which it is liable — which, however, are often greatly exaggerated,—is eminently favourable, as the tables of longevity and the habits of the people prove, both to life and enjoyment.

According to Professor Guy, the proportion of deaths to the population is, in

Austria	1 in 40.	Belgium	1 in 43.
Denmark	1 in 45.	England	1 in 46.
France	1 in 42.	Norway & Sweden	1 in 41.
Portugal	1 in 40.	Prussia	1 in 39.
Russia in Europe...	1 in 44.	Spain	1 in 40.
Switzerland	1 in 40.	Turkey	1 in 50.
United States	1 in 74	Upper Canada	1 in 102.
Lower Canada	1 in 92.	All Canada	1 in 98.

"The salubrity of the Province," remarks Mr. Hogan, from whom we have taken the above table, "is sufficiently proved by its cloudless skies, its elastic air, and almost entire absence of fogs. The lightness of the atmosphere has a most invigorating effect upon the spirits. The winter frosts are severe and steady, and the summer suns are hot, and bring on vegetation with wonderful rapidity. It is true that the spring of Canada differs much from the spring of many parts of Europe; but after her long winter the crops start up as if by magic, and reconcile her inhabitants to the loss of that which, elsewhere, is often the sweetest season of the year. If, however, Canada has but a short spring, she can boast of an autumn deliciously

mild, and often lingering on, with its Indian summer and golden sunsets, until the month of December.

"A Canadian winter, the mention of which some years ago, in Europe, conveyed almost a sensation of misery, is hailed rather as a season of increased enjoyment than of privation and discomfort by the people. Instead of alternate rain, snow, sleet and fog, with broken up and impassable roads, the Canadian has clear skies, a fine bracing atmosphere, with the rivers and many of the smaller lakes frozen, and the inequalities in the rough tracks through the woods made smooth by snow, the whole face of the country being literally macadamized by nature for a people as yet unable to macadamize for themselves."

4. *The constituents and character of its population.*

As a matter of course, its inhabitants share in the common characteristics of the races whence they have sprung—which include the leading peoples of Europe, those especially of the British Islands, and France and Germany—and natives of the United States. The circumstances in which they are placed—the constant demand on them for exertion during the earlier period of their residence in the country, the self-dependence they are called to exercise, connected with the measure in which they are thrown on one another's sympathy, and the hope amidst which they work—have a direct tendency to develope not a few of their better qualities. Even the variety of their previous modes of thought and action, though occasioning perhaps for a time some inconvenience, is a gain to them in the end by the contributions which it enables them to make severally to the common stock of ideas, and the habit which it produces of tolerance for unessential differences, consideration for one another's feelings, and appreciation of each other's virtues.

An incidental advantage of no small value, resulting from the variety of origin to which allusion has been made, is the sympathy which the new comer may look for from his countrymen, with the measure in which the privilege of association with them helps to make him feel himself at home. This is a source of comfort specially open to emigrants from Britain, France, and the neighbouring States.

Among the larger portion of our people there exists, alongside of the variety of origin alluded to, a homogeneousness which greatly facilitates their welding into one community, imparting to them. while the process is going on, a coincidence of feeling which makes living among them easy and pleasant, and secures their acting together in all matters of special moment.

The beneficial influence mutually exerted by the new-comer and the older resident on one another, is well brought out in the following passage of Mr. Hogan.

"It is a remarkable fact that the farmers of Upper Canada have opportunities of improvement, and of enlarging and correcting their views, beyond what are enjoyed by many of their class even in England. And this arises from the circumstance of the population being made up of so many varieties. The same neighbourhood has frequently a representative of the best farming skill of York. shire, of the judicious management and agricultural experiences of the Lothians, and of the patient industry and perseverance of Flanders. In a country so peopled, the benefits of travel are gained without the necessity of going away from home. Other countries, in fact, send their people to teach Canadians, instead of Canadians having to go to other countries to learn. A thousand experiences are brought to their doors, instead of their having to visit a thousand doors to acquire them. Nor is the advantage of this happy admixture of population altogether on the side of the Canadian; for whilst he gleans from the old countryman his skill and his science, he teaches him, in return, how to rely upon himself in emergencies and difficulties inseparable from a new country. how to be a carpenter when a storm blows down a door, and there is no carpenter to be had, and how to be an undismayed wheelwright when a waggon breaks down in the midst of a forest, and there is no one either to instruct or assist him. The one, in short, imparts to a comparatively rude people the knowledge and skill of an old and civilized country; the other teaches skilled labour how to live in a new land. The consequence is, the old countryman of tact becomes, in all that relates to self reliance and enterprise, a capital Canadian in a few years; whilst the Canadian, in all that pertains to skilful industry, becomes an Englishman."

The operation of the same fact, the mixed character of our population, on the culture of taste is shown in continuance of the above, but our space compels us to leave it unquoted. The principle may be applied more widely than it is by Mr. H. Its power is, in fact, coextensive with our whole thinking and working.

5. *Its institutions.*

No-where is a more perfect freedom enjoyed than here. Of a state of liberty more complete it would indeed be difficult even to form a conception. We live under laws of our own making or voluntary adoption, administered in courts established by ourselves, and by judges of our own appointing. The men by whom our general affairs are managed are chosen by ourselves and responsible to us for their conduct. Our municipal system gives the people a power in local matters which is supreme, and affords to the more ambitious and intelligent among them an opportunity of preparing themselves for the performance of higher duties, as well as of attracting the notice and securing the respect of the community. Of influence or station, there is nothing among us to which the poorest may not aspire.

"The general features of the municipal law of Upper Canada, and which, with some modifications suited to the different state of society in Lower Canada, may be stated as the system in force throughout the Province, are—

"The inhabitants of each county, city, town and township, are constituted corporations; their organization proceeding wholly upon the elective principle; and provision is made for the erection of new municipalities, as the circumstances of the country require, by their separation from those already existing. A complete system is created for regulating the elections, and for defining the duties of the municipalities and their officers. Their powers may be generally stated to embrace every thing of a local nature, including the opening and maintenance of highways, the erection of school houses, and the support of common and grammar schools; the provision of accommodation for the administration of justice, gaols, &c., and the collection of rates for their support, as well as for the payment of petty jurymen; granting shop and tavern licenses; regulating and prohibiting the sale of spirituous liquors; providing for the support of the poor; preventing the obstruction of streams; effecting drainage, both in the cities and county; inspection of weights and measures; enforcing the due observance of the Sabbath, and protection of public morals; establishing and regulating ferries, harbours, markets, &c.; abating nuisances; making regulations for and taking precautions against fires; establishing gas and waterworks; making police regulations; levying rates upon all real and personal property, including incomes, for all purposes; and, for certain objects, borrowing money; together with a great number of minor matters, essential for the good government of a community.

In educational advantages we know of no country so young that exceeds us. By few of that class are we even equalled. Our common schools, established on the best principles and taught by well-qualified and honourably-conducted teachers, offer to our youth at large the means of qualifying themselves for the intelligent and efficient performance of the duties awaiting them in their present social positions, or aiding them, it such be their wish, to raise themselves to such as are higher, either without cost or at a charge little more than nominal. For the obtaining of a still better culture our Grammar Schools, which are rapidly improving in character, offer all reasonable facilities; while our Colleges and Universities place professional training and instruction in the higher departments of learning and science within the reach of the possessors of moderate means, or such as, in the absence of these, may be disposed to maintain for a time a manly struggle for their own advancement.

From a valuable table (T) given in Dr. Ryerson's Report for 1861, we extract the following particulars illustrative of the educational progress of Upper Canada, between 1842 and 1861.

The number of common schools was, in 1842, 1,271; 1847, 2,727; 1852, 2,992; 1857, 3,631; 1861, 3,910. The pupils attending these numbered, in 1842, 65,978; 1847, 124,829; 1852, 179,587; 1857, 262,673; 1861, 316,287. Of Roman Catholic separate schools there are reported, for 1851, in which year they first appear in the returns, 16; 1857, 100; 1861, 109. There were, in 1845, 2,860 common school teachers employed; in 1850, 3,476; in 1855, 3,565; and in 1861, 4,336. There was paid for salaries of teachers of common and separate schools, erection and repair of school houses, libraries and apparatus, in 1850, $410,472; in 1855, $899,272; in 1861, $1,191,413. Of the schools thus reported there were 252 free in 1850; 1,211 in 1855; and in 1861, 2,903.

In 1842, there are supposed to have been in existence 25

county grammar schools. They numbered 32, in 1847; in 1852, 60; in 1857, 72; in 1861, 86. On these schools there were in attendance, in 1847, 1,000 pupils; in 1852, 2,643; in 1857, 4,073; in 1861, 4,766. The salaries paid the masters were, in 1855, the first year in which they are given separately, $46,255; in 1861, $71,034.

In 1842, we have reported, in addition to the above, 44 separate schools and academies (a supposed approximation); in 1847, 96; in 1852, 181; in 1857, 276; in 1861, 337. The number of pupils in these institutions was, in 1847, 1,531; in 1852, 5,684; in 1857, 4,073; in 1861, 4,766.

We had in operation, in 1847, six colleges, with an attendance of 700 students; in 1852, eight, with 751 students; in 1857, twelve, with 1,335 (approx.); 1861, thirteen, with 1,373 (approx.)

The amounts reported as paid for educational purposes, in Upper Canada were, in 1851, $599,980; in 1856, $1,326,992; in 1861, $1,476,107.

The following table, by J. G. Hodgins, LL.B., F.R.G.S., taken from "Eighty Years' Progress," &c. (p. 524), will give an idea of the educational advance of Lower Canada between 1852 and 1861.

Year.	Educational Institutions of all kinds.	Pupils.	Assessments and Fees.
1853	2,352	108,284	$165,848
1854	2,795	119,733	298,032
1855	2,868	127,058	249,136
1856	2,919	143,141	406,764
1857	2,986	148,798	424,208
1858	2,985	156,872	459,366
1859	3,199	168,148	498,436
1860	3,264	172,155	503,959
1861	3,345	180,845	526,219

As to religious privileges, we are also on the whole favourably situated. The right of judging for ourselves in these matters is universally recognized; and in the eye of the law we stand on an equality. The common denominations have all a place among us, so that we may each, if such be our desire, have the opportunity of connection, in the older portions of the country, at any rate, with those among whom we may have been brought up, or who may be preferred by us. Fair allowance being made for difference in circumstances, the means of instruction will compare favourably, as to character, in the greater part of these bodies, with those enjoyed by them elsewhere. Speaking generally, the usual forms of Christian exertion—the Sabbath school, Bible class, Bible, Tract and Missionary Societies, and kindred organizations—are found in healthful and vigorous operation among them. Notwithstanding their differing views, these denominations, moreover, dwell side by side in peace, treat each other with the courtesies common in other parts of the Christian world, and co-operate with one another for common objects, as much at least as is common in the lands whence they have come. The institutions for the relief of want and distress in its various forms, which usually follow in the wake of Christianity, have place and are carrying on their good work in our midst.

6. *The union which it offers of the advantages characteristic both of the older and the newer states of society.*

By selecting as their home the older parts of the country, those whose tastes would lead them to give the preference to the former may secure them in fair measure, provided they bring with them the necessary requisites in character, habits and means; while such as are willing to share the usual fortunes of the later, may calculate on the chances open to them in ordinary circumstances. Growth, with its attendant advantages, is in these chiefly a question of time and patience. At a much earlier age, and with much less of struggle than is requisite in older countries, the diligent and economical may hope to place themselves in a position of independence. As a general thing, the means of comfortable support is within the reach of the industrious, on conditions much less onerous than in these.

7. *Its relations and status.*

The emigrant to Canada has, in the fact of its forming part of the British empire, the guarantee of one of the most powerful nations of the earth for his protection against injury from without. In this respect, as in every other, the mother country does of course a right to expect that we shall make every reasonable effort to help ourselves. Should the necessity arise, this will be done; and being done, there need be feared on her part no failure.

Against the risk of any movement from within, which would interfere injuriously with him, he has equal assurance in the hearty loyalty and affectionate attachment of our people to the parent state, which would make them contemplate the prospect of separation with dislike, rather than pleasure.

The connection of Canada with Britain gives her also a standing, which, in addition to its agreeableness, is fitted to render important aid in her development. It tends to operate thus by the feeling of self-respect which it inspires and fosters, by the honours which it holds out to the ambitious the hope of sharing, and by the examples that are felt to be constantly inviting imitation.

Retaining, as he does, his connection with the land of his birth, the native of the Bri ish Islands who chooses Canada as his home, is saved from much of the feeling of expatriation which he would experience elsewhere. He finds himself but half a stranger, if even that. He looks with a pride, of which he was perhaps never previously conscious, on the old flag, as it floats over him; exults in his country's glories as his own; and finds a hymn in the National Anthem.

8. *The steadiness and satisfactoriness of its growth.*

A few particulars are all our space will admit in illustration of this.

The population of United Canada numbered in the year 1800, 240.000. It was in 1825, 581.920; by 1851. it had reached 1,842.265. In 1861, it amounted to 2,506,755. The advance in Upper Canada between 1825 and 1861 has been from 581,027 to 1,396,091—not much less than 800 per cent, in 36 years.

In 1831. the number of cultivated acres in the whole of Canada. Upper and Lower, was 2,884.345. It came up. in 1844. to 4,968,408; and in 1851, to 7,300.837. The returns for Lower Canada, for 1861, have not yet been published. In Upper anada alone, 6,051,619 are reported for that year.

Upper Canada had. in 1851. 99,906 occupiers of land. They numbered. in 1861, 131.983. It produced, in 1851, 12,682.550 bushels of wheat; 11,391,867 of oats; 9,982,186 of potatoes; 3,110,118 of turnips; of flax or hemp, 59,680 lbs.; 3,669.874 lbs. of maple sugar. Its produce of these articles was, in 1861 — wheat, 24,260,425 bushels; oats, 21.220,874; potatoes, 15,325,920; turnips, 18,206,959; flax or hemp. 1.225.934 lbs.; maple sugar, 6,370.605 lbs. The value of the live stock in Upper Canada was, in 1861, as much as $53,227,486; its agricultural implements, $11.280,347; its farms, $295,162,315. A similar progress will, we doubt not, be shown in Lower Canada, when its agricultural statistics for the year in question appear.

In 1808, the value of the entire trade of Canada was about $8.400,000. The value reached, in 1852—exports, $14,055,973; imports, $20,286,493; total, $34,342,466. In 1861, its imports amounted to $36,614,195; exports, $43,046,823; total, $79,661,013. The value of the trade with the United States alone was, in the last of these years, $35,455.815; the imports from that country reaching $21,069,388, and the imports to it $14,386,427.

In 1851, the net revenue yielded by the customs was $2,808,831; in 1861, $4,411,160. The value of books imported was, in 1850, $243,580; in 1861, $5.056,943.

On roads, navigation and railroads, the Province has expended as much as $60.000,000, over and above the interest in the latter of parties out of the country. There are in use at this moment between 1,800 and 1,900 miles of railway; besides 3,422 of electric telegraph, belonging to the Montreal Telegraph Company, which had, in 1861, a capital stock of $400,000 (to which it had advanced from $60.000, in 1847), employed 400 persons (35 in 1847), and conveyed 300,000 messages; the number conveyed in 1847 having been 33,000.

Our post offices have multiplied from 3, in 1766, to 69, in 1824; 601. in 1850, and 1.698, in 1860. The number of miles of e-tablished post roads was, in the first of these years, 170; in the second, 1.992; in the third, 7,595; and in the last, 14.202. The miles travelled were. in 1824, 309; in 1766, 616; in 1851, 2,287,000; in 1860, 5,712,000. In 1852, 3,700,000 letters were transmitted; in 1860, 9,000,000. The expenditure of the Post Office was, in the former of these years, $276,191, and its revenue $230,629; in the latter. its expenditure was $534,681, and its revenue $658.451. One hundred and ten thousand dollars additional is paid per annum, by way of subsidy, to railroads; and four hundred and sixteen thousand to steamships.

From the above, it will be seen that our growth has been rapid, steady and general; not coming by fits and starts, or confined in its sphere.

9. *Its prospects.*

It cannot fail, without fault on the part of its people, to continue growing and to become strong and prosperous and influential; for it has in itself, in its geographical position. and in its relations, all the elements of greatness. But such failure is not to be anticipated, as self-respect, interest and duty. unite in urging us to make the best of our position. The worst part of the struggle is over. To carry us to the height of any reasonable ambition, all that is necessary is perseverance for a moderate time in the self-denial and exertion of the past. with the careful avoidance of its errors, as far as they may be discovered.

The motive to throw in their lot with us, held out by such a state of things to those who may be contemplating change, is manifest. To witness progress is pleasant, how much more to share in it and to be made partakers of the advantages it yields.

10. *The common feeling of such as have made trial of the country.*

Few who have lived in it for any length of time, possessing the characteristics and pursuing the course necessary to success, would willingly exchange it for the lands whence they came. Nothing is more common than for those who visit their old homes, after a few year's residence in it, to feel impatient till they get back. Numbers who have left it with the intention of remaining at home, have returned to it, unable to enjoy themselves there. The freedom realized here from the burdensome restraints of older societies, and the social consideration which the deserving seldom fail to receive, help to explain the above state of feeling. In the fact of its existence the new comer. or the man contemplating coming, has fair promise and assurance that he will, in due time, feel himself one of us and at home among us.

The classes to which Canada will be found specially adapted are—

1. Farmers and parties accustomed to agricultural pursuits.

These may, if they bring moderate means with them, find cleared or uncleared farms, according to their taste, in most parts of the country, at prices moderate, though of course varying with quality of land, value of improvements, and location. Such as may be without the advantage of means may generally, if prepared to accept of reasonable wages, find employment and comfortable homes among our farmers. By satisfying themselves for a time with these. they gain an acquaintance with the country, the modes of working best suited to it. the most desirable locations, prices of land, &c., which will save them much to which they would be in danger otherwise of being subjected, and help them to work at advantage to themselves.

Though not in an equal degree, parties previously unaccustomed to agriculture, if disposed to devote themselves to it. may secure these advantages by the pursuance of the same course. Numbers are found all through the country, with good farms and in comfortable circumstances, who had their knowledge to acquire after their arrival. If possessed of the physical requisites and the power of adapting themselves to new circumstances, none who make up their minds to persevere, need despair, though, compared with the others, they must labour for a time under disadvantage.

2. Mechanics, those especially of the more common descriptions.

These may generally find employment in one part or another, indeed in almost any part of the Province, at fair wages, and within a reasonable time. If well-behaved, industrious and economical. they may hope to attain ultimately a good position both as to comfort and standing. Many of this class are to be met with in our cities, and even smaller towns and villages, living on their savings while yet comparatively young. Those of trades less common run, of course, more risk, though numbers even of these succeed in making themselves positions in the cities.

3. The possessors of spare means.

What they may be able and disposed to invest will afford this class much better returns here, without the adoption of any course involving wrong, than at home. They may also, if desirous of making themselves useful. obtain (provided they possess the necessary requisites) abundant means of doing so in harmony with their habits and tastes.

The things needful to success in Canada, without which none can hope for it, and with which none need despair of it, are—

1. Fair health, intelligence, and capacity for useful action.
2. Good principles and correct honourable habits.
3. Steady and patient perseverance.
4. A cheerful and hopeful spirit.
5. The blessing of God.

WILLIAM HALLEY,

83 BAY STREET, TORONTO,

DEALER IN

TYPES, PRESSES,

PRINTING INKS AND PRINTING MATERIALS,

HAS always on hand a large Stock of Messrs. MILLER & RICHARDS' (of Edinburgh and London) Scotch Cut Hard Metal Type, which he offers to Printers at a very low price for Cash. BOOK AND NEWS INK (the manufacture of A. B. FLEMING & Co., Leith) constantly in Stock. The *London Times*, and the leading Newspapers of Britain are printed with the Type and Ink here mentioned. W. H. is also Agent for the

PRINTING MACHINERY

Of Messrs. HUGHES & KIMBER, London, and would call attention to their "WHARFDALE" Machine, which is of a superior description and much cheaper than any Machine imported from the United States.

PRESSES OF EVERY DESCRIPTION,

Lithographic, Copperplate, and Bookbinders' Materials

SUPPLIED TO ORDER.

WILLIAM STEWARD,

Saddle,

HARNESS,

AND

TRUNK MAKER,

A Large and Well-assorted Stock always on hand.

142, cor. Yonge & Temperance St.

TORONTO.

LABELS.

Depot for Chemists' & Liquor Labels.

A large Stock always on hand.

NEW DESIGNS AND STYLES CONSTANTLY ADDED.

W. C. CHEWETT & CO.,

17 & 19 KING STREET EAST, TORONTO.

WHEELER & WILSON'S

NEW STRAIGHT NEEDLE, LOCK-STITCH

Sewing Machines,

THE FOREMOST IN THE MARKET.

Their claims to Notice are the following :—

1. The Machines are the result of more than a quarter of a century's manufacturing experience.

2. The rotary hook (in combination with the bobbin), runs more quietly and more rapidly than the shuttle, and is, consequently, more durable.

3. A finer needle can be used in these Machines, with a thread coarser than it is possible to use in any other ; a thread large enough to entirely fill the hole of the needle can be used, and thus a firmer and more beautiful stitch can be secured.

4. The needle is self-adjusting, and requires only to be placed in position.

5. Heavy seams can be crossed with them without trouble or delay.

6. As the bobbin is larger than the shuttle, it requires filling less frequently, and the under thread is more easily arranged than it can be on machines on which a shuttle is used.

7. The WHEELER & WILSON Machines have the needle-bars packed in felt, and thus prevents the oil soiling the work.

8. The bobbins do not need the application of oil ; a source of annoyance is thus avoided which *they* will appreciate who have been accustomed to soil their thread and work with oily shuttles, &c.

9. The great speed and durability of the WHEELER & WILSON Machines reduce the cost of production to MANUFACTURERS, and necessarily increase the earnings of OPERATIVES.

WHEELER & WILSON MANUFACTURING CO.

85 KING STREET WEST,

TORONTO, ONT.

☞ 282,812 ☜

GENUINE NEW YORK SINGER

SEWING MACHINES

SOLD LAST YEAR!!

200,000

MORE THAN WAS SOLD BY ANY OTHER COMPANY.

Unrivalled for the Range and Excellence of their Work.

BEWARE OF IMITATIONS!

SEE OUR BRASS TRADE MARK ON ARM OF MACHINE.

NONE OTHERS   ARE GENUINE.

THE SINGER MANUFACTURING CO.

TORONTO OFFICE, 22 Toronto Street.	BRANTFORD OFFICE, Y.M.C.A. Build'g
LONDON OFFICE, 222 Dundas Street.	WINDSOR OFFICE, 6 Dougall Bro. Block.
HAMILTON OFFICE, 94 King St. East.	GUELPH OFFICE, Masonic Block.
KINGSTON " Princess & Wellington Sts.	PORT HOPE OFFICE, Walton Street.

GEO. E. PATTERSON,

GENERAL ✳ ENGRAVER.

MANUFACTURER OF

Book cover stamps, ools, and rolls, brass signs, door plates, soap
dies, box makers stamps, biscuit and cork dies, shirt and
collar makers stamps, stencils, burning brands,
brass stamps, etc.

121 Church Street. - - TORONTO.

WILLIAM BROWN

44 & 46 WELLINGTON STREET EAST, TORONTO.

Keeps in Stock Sarven and other Wheels,

CARRIAGE HARDWARE.

RIMS, SPOKES, HUBS, SHAFTS, SPRINGS, AXLES,

Enamelled Top and Dash Leather, Rubber Cloth, Moquette.
Enamelled and Oil Cloth, Curled Hair and Moss,

CARRIAGE LAMPS, TRIMMINGS AND FURNISHINGS.

PUSHING A CLAIM.

"Hey, that's my umbrella! I know it by the blue patch in it."

"Well, I hope you won't claim my pants, too; for they have the same kind of a patch in them."

Great : African : Travellers

NEW BOOK PUBLISHED BY GEO. ROUTLEDGE & SONS, LONDON.

Great African Travellers from Mungo Park to Stanley, by C. R. LOW, with many illustrations, and portrait of Mr Stanley.

PRICE, - $2.60

ILLUSTRATION ON PAGE 474.

— FOR SALE BY —

THE COPP, CLARK CO., LTD., TORONTO.

BACKWOODS FARMER (*who has just finished the sign*):—I kinder like the idee, somehow 'r other. It has'r religous feelin' runnin' through it, an' at the same time means business!

HARPER'S YOUNG PEOPLE FOR 1891.

From Harper's Young People.—Copyright, 1890, by Harper & Bros.

A TALE OF WOE.

NOW IS THE TIME TO SUBSCRIBE.

Vol. XII Just Beginning.

From Harper's Young People.—Copyright, 1890, by
Harper & Brothers.

Subscription Price, - - - $2.00 a Year.

Postage Free to all Subscribers in the United States, Canada, or Mexico.

☞ Booksellers and Postmasters usually receive subscriptions. Subscriptions sent direct to the publishers should be accompanied by Post-office Money Order or Draft. When no time is specified, subscriptions will begin with the current Number.

Address: **HARPER & BROTHERS, Franklin Square, N. Y.**

BRITISH & FOREIGN IMPORTING HOUSE,

48 & 50 YONGE STREET, TORONTO.
455 ST. PAUL STREET, MONTREAL.

ROBERT WILKES,
WHOLESALE MANUFACTURERS' AGENT
IN CANADA, FOR

Connecticut Clocks.	Electro-Plated Spoons and Forks.
American Waltham Watches.	Electro-Plated Hollow Ware.
Nickelite Silver Spoons & Forks.	Sterling Silver Spoons and Forks.
Sheffield Table & Pocket Cutlery.	Enamelled Looking Glass Plate.
Gosnell's Perfumery & Brushes.	Swiss Watches, &c., &c., &c.

DIRECT IMPORTER OF

Musical Instruments.	Pipes.	Leather Goods.
Combs.	Musical Boxes.	Optical Goods.
Brushes.	Papier Machie Ware.	Toys.
Druggist's Sundries.	Perfumery.	Watches.
Cabinet Ware.	Stationer's Sundries.	Watch Materials.

And General Fancy Goods, &c., &c., &c.

COMMISSION MERCHANT FOR THE IMPORTATION OF

Hemp, Sisal, French Calf Skins, Bordeaux Goods, Rubber Goods, and any other legitimate articles of British or European manufacture.

SAMPLE ORDERS solicited from Merchants not visiting TORONTO or MONTREAL.

ROBERT WILKES.

PRINTED AT THE STEAM PRESS ESTABLISHMENT OF COPP, CLARK & CO., KING STREET EAST, TORONTO.

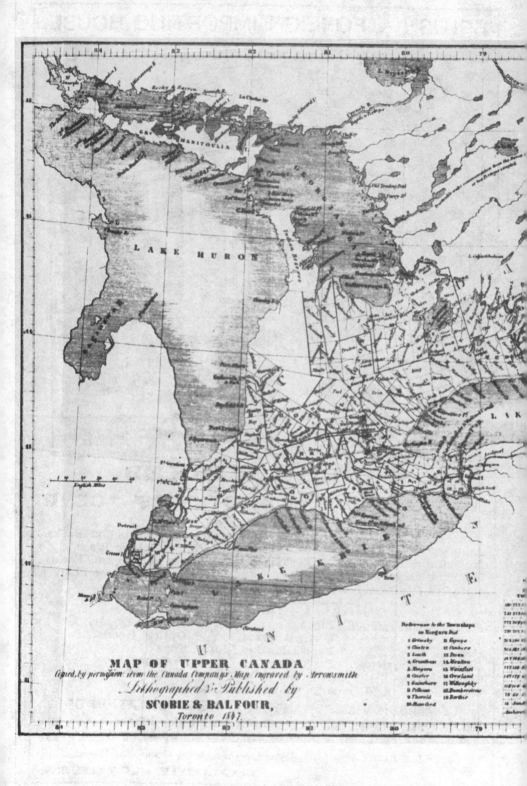

MAP OF UPPER CANADA

Copied, by permission, from the Canada Company's Map engraved by Arrowsmith

Lithographed & Published by

SCOBIE & BALFOUR,

Toronto 1847.

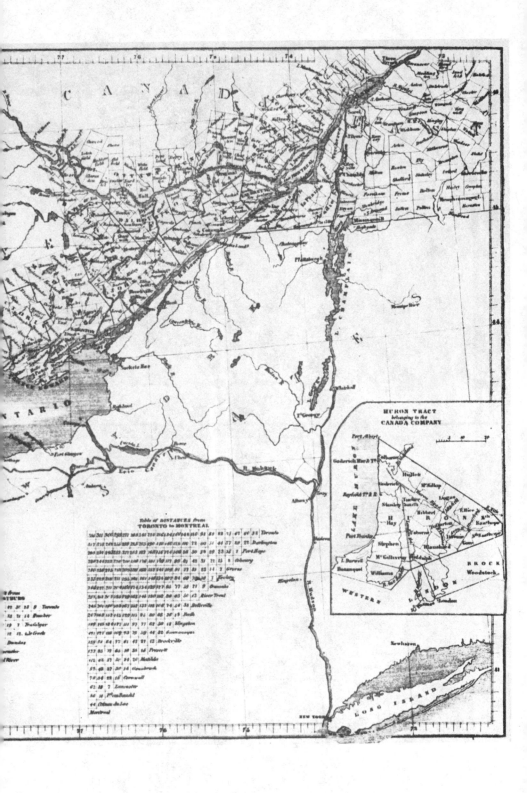

Table of DISTANCES from
TORONTO to MONTREAL

HURON TRACT
belonging to the
CANADA COMPANY

A Canadian Bestseller Since 1847!

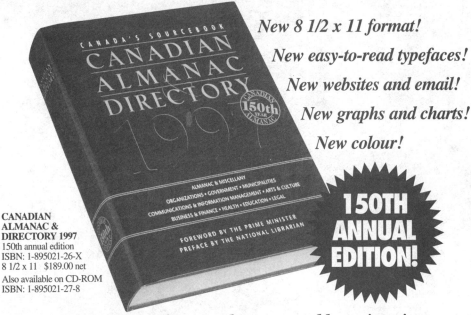

New 8 1/2 x 11 format!

New easy-to-read typefaces!

New websites and email!

New graphs and charts!

New colour!

150TH ANNUAL EDITION!

CANADIAN ALMANAC & DIRECTORY 1997
150th annual edition
ISBN: 1-895021-26-X
8 1/2 x 11 $189.00 net
Also available on CD-ROM
ISBN: 1-895021-27-8

"... this huge tome packs more than one could ever imagine between the covers of one book... It's a book of vast usefulness."

ROSALEEN DICKSON, 'HILL TIMES', OTTAWA

Canada's authoritative source book. This national directory and guide gives you well over 100,000 names and addresses of government officials and contacts throughout the network of Canadian institutions. The volume contains ten directories in one. Sections provide full directories of Financial Institutions, Media—all print and broadcast, libraries and museums, hospitals, transportation and education (boards, universities and colleges, private schools, etc.).

A major section with its own keyword index covers federal and provincial ministries and departments with chief officials, acts administered, etc. We even provide a major trading partner equivalency guide to match up department activities in each country. All municipalities are listed with key information. Major cities are presented in some depth. A complete legal directory lists courts and judges, judicial officials and law firms.

A wealth of general information provides national statistics on population, employment, CPI, imports and exports, etc. National awards and honours are presented with forms of address, precedence and Canadian symbols. Postal information, weights, measures and distances and other useful charts are incorporated. Complete almanac information includes perpetual calendars and five-year holiday planners. Fully indexed.

ABBREVIATIONS • ASSOCIATIONS AND SOCIETIES • BROADCASTING AND COMMUNICATIONS • BUSINESS STATISTICS
CHURCH AND RELIGIOUS ORGANIZATIONS • COMMERCE AND FINANCE • CULTURAL DIRECTORY • EDUCATION DIRECTORY
ELECTORAL DISTRICTS • FOREIGN AND INTERNATIONAL CONTACTS • GEOGRAPHIC INFORMATION • GOVERNMENT DIRECTORY
GOVERNMENT QUICK REFERENCE • HEALTH AND HOSPITALS • HISTORICAL AND GENERAL INFORMATION
LEGAL AND JUDICIAL DIRECTORY • POSTAL INFORMATION • TOURISM AND TRANSPORTATION

FOR MORE INFORMATION OR TO ORDER CALL 1-800-815-9417

COPP CLARK PROFESSIONAL LTD., 200 ADELAIDE STREET WEST, 3RD FLOOR, TORONTO, ONTARIO M5H 1W7 (416) 597-1616